Practising Videojournalism

If you are excited by the possibilities of videojournalism then this is the book for you.

In a world where newspapers have websites running video, broadcasters are offering programming online, independent internet channels are springing up and companies want to run video on the web, the moving image is central to the ways in which we communicate. This essential text explains how to combine your writing ability with video skills and gives practical advice on the whole filming process. From researching and pitching ideas, to filming using a small video camera, this text gives invaluable tips on framing shots, doing pieces to camera and interviewing. A further section looks at editing, how to organise material and the use of software by independents.

Videojournalists working in broadcast newsgathering offer advice on filming and working practices and for the first time you can learn about the history of videojournalism. Vivien Morgan discusses the importance of 1989 as a turning point when journalists picked up small video cameras and went out to document turbulent events throughout the world, leading to the birth of a new style of newsgathering: intimate, portable, quick and economic.

Looking to the future, the book provides valuable guidance on how to work with new media, defining blogging, podcasting RSS feeds, user-generated content and mobile videocasting.

Vivien Morgan has over 25 years' experience in broadcast TV and print media. She is a pioneer of videojournalism for TV news, as well as being a producer/director on the first dedicated Business TV programme. She has taught broadcast and video journalism, writing for news and new media at a number of UK universities. She currently works as a Communication Project Consultant and Media Trainer.

Practising Videojournalism

Vivien Morgan

Routledge
Taylor & Francis Group

LONDON AND NEW YORK

First published 2008
by Routledge
2 Park Square, Milton Park, Abingdon, Oxon OX14 4RN

Simultaneously published in the USA and Canada
by Routledge
270 Madison Ave, New York, NY 10016

Routledge is an imprint of the Taylor & Francis Group, an informa business

© 2008 Vivien Morgan

Typeset in Sabon by
HWA Text and Data Management, Tunbridge Wells
Printed and bound in Great Britain by
TJ International Ltd, Padstow, Cornwall

British Library Cataloguing in Publication Data
A catalogue record for this book is available from the British Library.

Library of Congress Cataloging-in-Publication Data
Morgan, Vivien, 1949–
    Practising videojournalism / Vivien Morgan.
        p. cm.
    Includes bibliographical references and index.
    1. Video journalism. 2. Digital video–editing. 3. Video recordings–
Production and direction. I. Title.
    TR895.59–dc22
    778.59–dc22

                                                                    2007006061

ISBN10: 0–415–38665–9 (hbk)
ISBN10: 0–415–38666–7 (pbk)
ISBN10: 0–203–94484–4 (ebk)

ISBN13: 978–0–415–38665–4 (hbk)
ISBN13: 978–0–415–38666–1 (pbk)
ISBN13: 978–0–203–94484–4 (ebk)

Contents

Illustrations

Preface

Do you use your mobile, text people, check your e-mails and spend a few hours every day online? Do you sometimes use a video camera and then download the pictures onto your pc, or perhaps do the same with a digital still camera? Am I describing your life? You can do all these activities simply since the arrival of broadband on the internet. This book discusses how this change has impacted on communication methods and our way of life in general and specifically the rise of videojournalism. It also tells the exciting history of how small video cameras came into our lives – not just in journalism, but for our general use. This is put in a social, historical and political context, along with detailed discussion of technological developments. There was a moment in time when three events coincided: the small Hi8 video camera came onto the market, momentous events began in Europe in 1989 and the pioneer VJs or videojournalists were ready to record. A new style of newsgathering, more discreet, intimate, portable, quick and economic, evolved to record the Berlin Wall as it came down and the dramatic changes in Eastern bloc countries, followed by the USSR, as they opened up in succession. More than that, these VJs were able to travel all over the world, to Africa and to South East Asia too, to record conflicts, famines and political and social changes, cheaply and easily with no more than a small video camera. They brought back pictures from countries people had never seen pictures of before such as Albania, Romania and the Central Asian 'stans.

We forget how fast something new is absorbed and becomes part of our culture. User-generated content, UGC, or citizen reporting, for example, is now accepted; people using their mobile phones and hand-held devices to record images and so contribute to breaking news coverage.

Local and community TV has also emerged, with VJs operating in a new way, giving students of videojournalism work outlets in the fast-developing world of new media.

There are chapters on newsgathering, media ownership and tips on researching, filming, script-writing and pitching ideas. One chapter is dedicated to new media and defines blogging, podcasting, RSS feeds and mobile videocasting.

Finally the book tries to see what the future might bring. Today we have newspapers with websites running video, multi-media platforms for broadcasters, independent internet channels and not just media organisations but all sorts of organisations gearing up for multi-media.

If you are excited by the possibilities of video or want to include it in your skills, this book will help you learn more about videojournalism as a whole.

If you would like to ask questions, discuss or contribute thoughts please go to my blog practisingvideojournalism.wordpress.com.

Acknowledgements

I'd like to thank the following people who agreed to interviews: Andy Benjamin, Giles Croot, Dan Damon, Will Daws, Nancy Durham, Nicholas Guthrie, John Ive, Gareth Jones, Sue Lloyd-Roberts, Ron McCullagh, Laura McMullan, Charles Morgan, Mike Morris, Ian O'Reilly, Sue Owen, Tim Parker, Stuart Ratcliffe, Vin Ray, Gwynne Roberts, Vaughan Smith, Rick Thompson.

Plus: Carolyn Wyndham and Bob Evans for shelter; Anne Furniss, Tiddy Rowan and Siri Harris for their support.

1 Towards a definition of videojournalism

So what is videojournalism? The term originally emerged to describe a style of filming where a journalist used a small lightweight video camera to single-handedly film and report a story, instead of working with a crew consisting of a cameraperson, soundperson and even lighting technician or 'sparks'. Videojournalism was a term that was devised *after* it had become a practice and once broadcasters recognised it (see Chapter 3 on VJ pioneers). Now, while the principal definition remains, the application is much wider and the term is actually being used to describe all filming using small video cameras.

Videojournalism keeps being re-invented and keeps moving with technological changes. It is also growing in demand as a skill which is good news for students and others looking to work as VJs. Newspapers which are filming video stories for their websites for example can now send their print journalists to a newly-created videojournalism course run by the Press Association or the Thomson Foundation. Traditional broadcasters continue to employ professional news camera people to film video for their newsgathering operations but a percentage of content is coming from non-professional or 'citizen' reporters who happen to record an event live as it happens. They are also rolling out local TV stations that provide community coverage, helped by the financial viability of using VJs and internet technology, namely broadband. For every website that wants to stream video either live or recorded, a videographer of some description is needed.

There are lone VJs or videojournalists who report/shoot/edit news stories for broadcast or local TV on a daily basis; there are practising TV journalists and correspondents who have the VJ skills to shoot video but do not always work alone, nor do they edit their material; there are videographers who capture events using small dv (digital video) cameras but whose primary role is as print journalists; there are features and documentary makers who shoot video; and there are citizen journalists who capture events using dv cameras or mobile phones who are also VJs.

Confused? Well, the media landscape in which people are now working demands multi-media skills and journalists are merely responding to the needs for capturing content for news or other broadcast genres. Can you remember a time before you had a credit card or a mobile phone? Think about how you now expect instant cash and instant calling or texting. How you also expect to catch the latest news on anything from celebrity gossip to sports to events listings, weather and traffic updates: online, via your mobile phone or hand-held device or on TV via a rolling news programme. Some of this is text information; a good deal of it though is in the form of video and the demand for content is growing, as is the discipline now called videojournalism. The immediate transmission and delivery of news items and events via various platforms but especially via the web, has brought about the 'unbundling of news'. This means it is no longer delivered only at specific times and bulletins, but continuously. Also the kind of news being broadcast via the web or linear TV has changed. Interactivity is already gathering pace, with non-journalists sending in video material, providing what has been termed 'user-generated images' of the 7 July 2005 bombings in central London for example. Traditional broadcasters, internet channels, search engines such as Google and Yahoo! and every sector that has a website presence (including newspapers) are requesting feedback and comment and allowing for the posting of video, audio and print on their portals. The consumer rules because the choices are wider, and where they go, the advertisers and the money follow. Technology is focused on providing ever better communication networks, which in turn are allowing the democratisation of the media.

Videojournalism is being pushed centre stage into this scenario, beyond newsgathering, to encompass an increasingly wide range of end-users of video content. So within the space of 25 years, the discipline has moved far from its roots to become a commonly used communication tool. Not only that, but it is a skill that most people who have grown up in the so-called 'video' age have mastered. Picking up a video camera or mobile phone to record images and then download them onto a computer or upload them onto the internet for use or display is easily done. Helped by ever simpler software, we are all using it, even if we are not professionals; we download our digital photos and then upload them onto sites for friends, family or the world to share. Pictures, moving or still, are part of our everyday lives as entertainment or as part of work. This is why the BBC in its new five-year plan, called Creative Future and launched in 2006, talks about 'knowledge building', not just newsgathering; the provision of all kinds of information that is topical, relevant and entertaining, that affects our lives. Google Earth, for example, uses satellite technology to let you explore the world and zoom in on places, capture images and feel very much that it is your, or our, universe. It is a simple, empowering tool and also educational and fun to use.

The web page Hot Zone, on Google, has Kevin Sites as a VJ reporting from every war zone. A year-long project, it could roll for ever and is a good example of videojournalism. Sites himself says, 'to me [videojournalism is] this strange juncture of old and new. It's a nexus of storytelling and latest-edge technologies, and delivering it on a platform which is probably the newest of all the mediums'.

Delivering on news platforms are companies advertising their services or streaming video of, say, their annual report from their website; or it could be an independent internet channel such as Current TV which is empowering others. Material can be uploaded on the 'outer-net' and watched. Of course there are the online 'star' sites like MySpace.com and YouTube.com that allow and provide for the showing of videos made by anyone, along with blog servers also now accommodating vlogs or video blogs.

Question: are non-journalists who record and post videos onto sites or send them to broadcasters, videojournalists? They recorded images of the 7 July bombings, for example, on their mobile phones and some sold those images for profit. Were the amateur videographers who ran to their cupboards or drawers and pulled out their video cameras or happened to have them with them, and recorded for posterity the planes hitting the World Trade Center in New York on 11 September 2001 also videojournalists? Are the US soldiers filming video of their bombings and incidents in Iraq and then posting them on the internet on YouTube.com and Ogrish.com, videojournalists?

Before deciding whether or not the 'journalism' part of the term matters, let us take a look at how it all began.

The early days of videojournalism

The idea of non-professional camera people shooting video was a seed carried along by the wind of technological change, finally coming to rest with the launch of the Hi8 video cameras. This marks the beginning of the modern history of videojournalism dating from 1986 when Sony brought out its first popular camera. There were other models, the Video8 and Super8, that preceded the Hi8 model but they failed to capture the public and professionals' imagination. (This is discussed further in the next chapter on technology development.) The Hi8 camera was for the consumer market, it was considerably smaller than the professional ones being used at that time, it could be hand-held easily and had simple button controls that anyone could work. There was a built-in microphone and most importantly the tapes were small, compact and easy to put in the camera. The more difficult task was transferring the recorded footage or 'rushes' for editing. Sony and other manufacturers of course had no idea how these cameras were going to be taken up by newsgatherers and eventually used in a different way. I personally used one for secretly filming particular people arriving at an airport in 1987 for a documentary I was producing. For the same film I employed a two-person team using a Hi8 camera to pose as tourists and shoot footage in a difficult environment.

Timing is of the essence when launching a new product and in this case when the wave of political change began to sweep across the former Eastern bloc countries, the former Soviet Union or USSR, moving eastward through

Central Asia from 1989, the small cameras came into their own. Freelance journalists invested in them, together with those seeing the opportunity afforded by these small cameras. Dan Damon (now a BBC radio presenter) set up his own company based in Budapest, Hungary to cover events. He used a group of Hungarians to travel into East Germany before the Berlin Wall fell and then to other closed countries using the cameras and to bring back footage in a number of ways on the new small cassettes. The Romanian Revolution of December 1989 marked for many, including myself, a turning point where unique coverage was shot by small cameras. Frontline News was set up in a hotel in Bucharest, Christmas 1989 as a result of their cameraman Rory Peck capturing the best moments of the fall of the dictator Nicolae Ceausescu. The new company's policy, they resolved, was to use Hi8 cameras to cover breaking news stories. Why? Well, as one of the founders, Vaughan Smith, explained,

> Rory Peck had already used a Hi8 camera in Jalalabad in 1989 when fighting was going on between the mujahedin and government forces. He got the footage and the TV news companies unquestionably bought it because no one else had got it – so there was a market for it.

The existence of a market for such material was proved again by the sale of footage of events in Bucharest. For Frontline the First Gulf War in 1991 was further vindication, if any was needed, that small cameras could get results – both visual and financial. In fact on the back of that war another video company Insight News was set up, also focussing on providing news material of events that the bigger companies could not cover.

In my first encounter with Hi8, at the start of a number of years as a VJ (up to the present day), it was the story that demanded the technology. We all proved that we could capture footage that could not be captured by other means. From Channel 4 News in 1989, I joined Sue Lloyd-Roberts, an already well-known reporter at ITN (Independent TV News), on the News at Ten programme. She had been introduced to Hi8 filming by Gwynne Roberts, a freelance ex-Reuters journalist, on their trip to Armenia (see Chapter 3 on video journalist pioneers).

It was the winter of 1989, just before the revolution, when we went to Romania. It was still a closed country with a dictatorial President, Nicolae Ceausescu. We went posing as independent tourists on a skiing trip. Our aim was to film and prove the destruction of countless villages around the capital Bucharest that had been carried out to make way for Ceausescu's vision of a modern Romania. We were equipped with the first Hi8 camera that ITN had purchased. Sue was a staff reporter, but allowed to use it as management had decided that it would only be necessary to negotiate with the unions if we returned with any useable footage of any news value. We managed to record and capture footage of the destroyed villages, interviews and also general shots of the capital and the new-look Bucharest that the world had yet to see. Our shots were rarely steady as we were followed by the secret police, called the Securitate, everywhere and were arrested at least nine times in as many days. We called it 'wobbly scope'. The images on those first cameras were rather fuzzy and our shots had a distinct greenish tinge. We did not have time to use zoom as the shots were snatched, and many were wide shots. Only one interview in a more controlled interior location was better, but it was still hand-held. We paid scant attention to sound.

As other videojournalists discovered around this time, the importance of the pictures outweighed the quality. The tapes were smuggled out and our report sold worldwide, with us keeping ownership of the footage, making it worthwhile financially.

So a new equation emerged: small = covert = portability = opportunity = results = financial gain. Match this with the adventuring spirit of journalists seeking to break the mould of the old newsgathering methods and the result was something original and unique.

So how does the style of filming differ so radically from traditional methods?

Table 1.1 defines the different ways a story can be covered and shows quite clearly the distinction between professional broadcast journalism as practised by the broadcast companies and others. The former have the finance, infrastructure, editorial policy and guidelines in place to approach stories in a complex but organised fashion. Their guiding principle is to get the facts right and to act as gatekeepers as well as newsgatherers, conscious of their remit to provide impartial and factual reporting of events and their national and international impact.

The local VJ has to provide a daily story for a small local broadcast area, and some of the stories may be picked up for regional news bulletins. The focus is on human interest stories and those that are not necessarily 'hard' news but still make an impact within the community. The radio and TV editor is the gatekeeper and a producer checks the scripts, shots and editorial approach. While objectivity is still important, the need for a balanced report is not necessarily paramount. The freelance VJ is only checked on editorially and visually much later in the newsgathering process, so the focus and content of the story is very much decided by them alone. The newspaper VJ has the editorial back-up of the news desk and editors and is not required either to edit or re-write the piece. An online team does this and is also under online editorial control.

To try and refine the definition of VJ practice further, let us look at the coverage of a fictitious event. This shows clearly the way different people can pick up video cameras or even a mobile phone and record an event. This is a present reality.

Time: 09.00 in a London newsroom.

Scenario: An agency newswire flashes a story onto the newsroom screens of the production team.

Table 1.1

Methodology	Broadcast journalism	Local TV VJ	Freelance VJ	Print VJ
Choosing a story	In the newsroom with the editorial team. The editor or producer of the day helps make the choice, or okays a story that is proposed.	The VJ finds a story each day that is okayed by the producer.	The videojournalist decides alone about following a story. It can be pitched to a broadcaster and is not always pre-sold for foreign stories but usually is for domestic ones.	In the newsroom with the editorial team. The news editor of the day helps make the choice, or okays a story that is proposed.
Timing	The reporter knows which bulletin s/he is aiming for depending on the programme that s/he works for. Rolling 24-hour news is different from the one, six or ten o'clock news bulletins.	The schedule is defined, a story must be shot and edited each day and finished by 17.00 hours. So speed is essential.	Being able to work economically, to cover a story on the day, edit it for the same day and produce a story of an acceptable standard. The selling point of the foreign exercise is to 'scoop' the broadcast news teams and get to inaccessible places and people. Time is not critical if the story demands spending days or weeks covering it and knowing you have something exclusive.	The reporter knows that s/he has to make the deadline for the print story, but also has to shoot stills and video for the online story, the latter to be uploaded as soon as possible.
Filming	This is done by a professional cameraperson and sometimes a soundperson as well, while	This is done by the VJ. The style of filming is by their description looser, often hand-held and more	This is done by the VJ. The style of filming is often dictated by the circumstances but is not constrained by any	This is done by the VJ.

	the reporter works on the storyline, finds people to interview, thinks about locations and what is needed for the piece visually.	close up and intimate. Tripods are used, especially during longer interviews. Broadcasters demand steady shots of sufficient duration for editing and the VJ needs these too.	traditional or 'set' shots, although tripods are used, especially during longer interviews. Broadcasters demand steady shots of sufficient duration for editing and the VJ needs these too.	
Camera	Sony Betacam or DVcam.	Z1 or PD170 or even the smaller PD150.	Z1, Canon XLR1, PD170, VX2000 series.	Z1, Canon XLR1, PD170, VX2000 series.
Writing	The reporter writes the script, chooses the soundbites and usually does a piece to camera.	The VJ writes the script and manages a piece to camera.	The VJ writes the script and manages a piece to camera.	The VJ writes the piece. Depending on the story, whether it is reporter-led or is just pictures for the website version, s/he will adapt the written piece for the video version.
Editing	A videotape editor will normally cut the piece, but sometimes the reporter will cut it themselves on the new digital editing desktop system.	The piece is edited alone.	The piece is edited alone.	The piece is edited by an online video editor.

(continued ...)

Table 1.1 ... continued

Methodology	Broadcast journalism	Local TV VJ	Freelance VJ	Print VJ
Commentary	The reporter writes and voices the commentary.	The reporter writes and voices the commentary.	Sometimes the VJ writes and voices the commentary, depending on the programme's policy. If sold to other countries, the piece is usually revoiced in the national language so only a guide track or script is offered.	The reporter writes and voices the commentary if needed.
Editorial viewing and 'gatekeeping'	The piece is okayed by the producer of the day or someone who holds editorial control and checks for legal, ethical, language, objectivity, focus and other potential problems.	The piece is okayed by the producer of the day or someone who holds editorial control and checks for legal, ethical, language, objectivity, focus and other potential problems.	Before transmission the piece will have to be checked by a programme producer who has editorial control and looks for legal, ethical, language, objectivity, focus and other potential problems.	The piece is okayed by the online news editor or someone who holds editorial control and checks for legal, ethical, language, objectivity, focus and other potential problems.

Story: There has been a freak tidal wave that has hit the south coast of England, sweeping inland for about one mile. Taking everyone by surprise, the devastation has been huge. Emergency services are racing to the scene.

The news advisory says updates will follow.

Action: The news editor decides with or without a conference with his team how to cover this. The location is looked at, the availability of local crews, the time it would take to get a London crew of reporter and cameraperson there, and how they would feed their pictures and story back in time to make the early bulletins or to go live onto a rolling 24-hour news channel. A reporter is assigned the story, s/he makes a few calls to local newspapers, makes contact with the cameraperson and they get everything under way within an hour.

Scenario 2: At 09.00 the same story is reported on local radio as a newsflash.

A freelance videojournalist living in Brighton immediately looks at the map and realises that the wave has hit just some 30 minutes away by car. S/he grabs a laptop, a camera kit that comprises a Z1 Sony camera, stick and clip microphones, and a tripod, and heads out the door. Within half an hour s/he is at the edge of the wave's path of destruction and begins filming. While doing this a second smaller but still large wave follows. The videojournalist is there and gets the moment of impact as the wave hits and surges inland. S/he continues to film and by 10.30 has some unique shots. Calling the news broadcast channels, BBC, Sky, ITV News, ITN and local Meridian, s/he is able to alert them to the fact that s/he has this footage, can sell it to the highest bidder and then send it down a broadband line using a wireless connection point for connecting the laptop. S/he can then go back and continue getting more interviews and other pictures.

Scenario 3: The local newspaper in Brighton has sent out its reporter along with a small video camera to report on the scene. The reporter arrives later than the videojournalist and so misses the second wave. However s/he manages to get some good shots for the paper's website and also sends them back via a laptop.

Scenario 4: The school in the path of the wave has one class out in the playground. As the wave approaches one of the children pulls out his mobile phone, which he should have handed in, and starts filming the wave's approach. Ignoring the shouts of the teacher to come inside he continues filming and then runs for his life.

Scenario 1 revisited: The broadcast team get to the disaster scene within two hours. They are delayed by the emergency services who have cut off the main roads into the area and have to work hard to get through the emergency cordons. By 13.00 they have managed to start filming. The satellite truck arrives shortly afterwards having had less far to travel. The reporter manages to feed live into the lunchtime news bulletin. He has missed the second wave and the early shots of the wave's destruction, but by now the channel has got the videojournalist's footage that includes floating bodies and the second wave hitting. The quality is acceptable; the shots are good. The only wobbly bits are when the second wave takes the videojournalist by surprise but this adds to the impact of what is being seen.

The staff reporter continues to feed updates in over the rest of the day and then repairs to a local newsroom in Brighton to package a piece and send it 'down the line' via a usually fixed link to the London newsroom. The 2-minute piece runs on the early evening and late evening bulletins. It includes a piece to camera and 'vox pops' with people at the scene, as well as soundbites from emergency services.

Scenario 2 revisited: The videojournalist has contacted the agencies and sold on the original footage. One foreign network channel has asked for more pictures and to stay on the story for the next couple of days. The videojournalist also uploads some of the pictures onto his/her website. This results in some more sales.

Scenario 3 revisited: Back at the newspaper office, the reporter's pictures have been uploaded immediately and used as a still for the front 'page' of the website as well as being cut down for a video, for streaming or run on demand. The stills are also used for that evening's newspaper front page story that the reporter will write or contribute to.

Scenario 4 revisited: That evening when watching the early news the schoolboy sees the appeal for any footage, contacts Sky News and sends them his shots. They make the late evening bulletin. Shaky but clear even when enlarged, the pictures show the oncoming wave up close. His pictures are termed 'user-generated images', his name is not mentioned and he did not ask for a fee.

Outcome scenario 1: While the broadcast channel is slower off the mark, in the end they manage comprehensive reporting of the piece by buying and incorporating the action footage of the videojournalist. The staff reporter is accredited with praise for the piece and is seen onscreen.

Outcome scenario 2: The videojournalist has been lucky in selling the footage. The foreign network wants a packaged or edited piece, along with a script and a guide track voiced by the VJ. The final report will be voiced in Dutch.

Outcome scenario 3: The newspaper reporter has managed to get the pictures and a story out on the website and on the front page of that evening's newspaper. He was lucky enough to find a little girl plus her puppy being rescued from the water.

Outcome scenario 4: The schoolboy has been praised by his schoolmates but reprimanded by the headmaster for risking his life. He thinks he might like to be a journalist.

Conclusion: They are not all videojournalists. The TV and print reporters and the VJ have been able to write about the event and have practised their craft of journalism. The schoolboy is not a journalist; he is just a videographer.

Videojournalism *is* then about the filming *as well as* the journalism. This means that anything outside this definition, the recording of video that is used by broadcasters for news and other programming, the recording of video for uploading to the internet whether on corporate or personal websites, is videography. So the schoolboy in our imaginary scenario is a videographer, the US soldiers in Iraq are videographers, and the so-called 'citizen journalists' are videographers; not journalists.

Moreover, videojournalism is now seen by some as a true *genre* of filmmaking.

Its emergence has been called the 'Bauhaus of television news pictures' (*Videojournalism Today* http://www/viewmagazine.tv/videojournalism_conf.html), a shift from the old to a dramatic new style of filming, the birth of a new 'medium'. It has certainly brought with it a new way of filming, hand-held, close-up and intimate, with movement and a 'rough and ready' feel to the footage. It is raw, as un-edited film footage used to be called, and unpredictable in its achievements, perhaps because the method or style of filming was developed by operators such as those journalists who had not shot before and were working in difficult situations or others (ex-soldiers in the case of Frontline and Nick Downey, see Chapter 3). So they shot what they could, where they could. Uninhibited by conventions that governed professional crews, these operators found a freedom and creative impulse that was determined by circumstance and defined or limited to a certain extent by the cameras.

> It gave people like me great freedom. I've always loved working with a crew and still do. But shooting your own stories allows you to be fleeter of foot and more flexible than a larger team. You've only got yourself to sort out and to please when you're on assignment. A lot of crews I'd worked with up 'til then were high-maintenance types and often a pain on foreign jobs.
>
> (Gareth Jones, a VJ since 1991, now BBC Wales)

The original news-crewing Gareth mentions was three plus one: reporter plus camera, sound and lights. Although as one news cameraman put it,

> lighting men tried to get on every job but usually only made it to about 50 per cent. They used to carry a large battery plus a 'hand-basher' light and tried to make themselves useful, usually as the team jester.
>
> (Charles Morgan, former ITN cameraman)

As ENG (electronic newsgathering) technology came in, the cameras became more light-sensitive and had camera lights that could be fixed to the top of the camera so the lighting man lost out even further. He was followed by the sound recordist, although much later on in the 1990s when again sound improvements meant it was easier for a cameraman to do sound too, helped by the reporter. Union negotiations and pay issues as discussed in the next chapter were also driving these changes. Today it is usually a single cameraperson who goes out with a reporter; although this is not the case on features, drama and other types of filming, only for newsgathering. Again there are exceptions: if you are doing a two-camera interview, say with a government minister, then a sound recordist could be included.

For the main broadcasters such as ABC, NBC, CBS, CBC, BBC and so on, 'one plus one', it is argued, continues to allow the technicians and journalists the best way of capturing events. As Vin Ray, Head of the BBC Journalism School, affirms

> Thus far videojournalism is not challenging mainstream newsgathering. For network BBC the majority of stuff is still done by crews. It has never been regarded as an 'on the day' activity, always for slightly longer foreign projects and pointed to the cheaper end of the market.

Note his use of the term 'thus far', for nothing in the future about video use is certain. One American businessman, Michael Rosenblum, used the cheapness argument to turn the medium into a commercial enterprise. He argued that it could help broadcasters and channels reduce their costs dramatically by turning all their journalists into VJs. It is interesting to note that Rosenblum has been paid to train hundreds of people as VJs globally, but the traditional format for newsgathering by the big TV companies and agencies has remained. Channel One in London was a short-lived operation set up by Rosenblum, staffed by VJs who used professional cameras but were solo journalists. The output was on cable and the failure to secure a wider audience caused its demise, but not before it had seen a number of young aspirant camera operators and journalists pass through, many of whom are broadcast stalwarts today.

The BBC's decision to train some 600 journalists on PDP (personal development programme) courses where they learned self-operating camera techniques for filming programmes, not just news, has failed to generate sufficient enthusiasm for them to maintain their new skills, or implement them. The time lapse between doing the course and then the opportunity or need to put the skills to use has been cited by many as a reason why they have forgotten how to use a camera – or else they prefer to concentrate on the journalism and leave the technical side to someone else.

While recent local TV experiments by all the UK broadcasters, ITV, BBC and Sky, have used only VJs, the pilots have shown that the stress of producing a daily report is high. Having visited and watched the operation and talked to the VJs, it would seem it is hard to maintain the output. A lower output or a larger team would be better, thus increasing costs, which might nullify the rationale for using VJs in the regions where budgets are considerably lower for all broadcasters. The concern by many in the industry is that this is exploitative TV and that somewhere the journalism and quality gets diluted, and that this is inevitable.

> I have always been aware of the technology as a double-edged sword, liberating journalists on the one hand, but allowing cost-cutters to exploit us. I always said videojournalism was great for features because you have more time, but bad if managers tried to use it for on-the-day news. It may save on camera-operators but it can put too much pressure on VJs and lead to diminishing quality.
>
> (Gareth Jones)

The quality argument is one which is standard when fighting against VJs in newsrooms. As the small cameras improve and communication technology makes sending material back so fast even easier, this argument is proving harder to justify.

Videojournalism has its roots in the past. It is a hybrid that has emerged from a number of different disciplines or work practices, in particular from photojournalism where stills photographers have for over a century been going out to cover news stories, wars and social or cultural events for newspapers, working in the same way as the modern VJ. Essentially the photojournalist works alone on capturing the images. Photojournalism is a particular form of journalism (i.e. the collecting, editing and presenting of news material for publication or broadcast) that creates images in order to tell a news story. It is usually understood to refer only to still images, and to refer largely to serious news stories. Videojournalism can also be linked to the way the newsreels were shot and produced. Pathe and Movietone News were just two of the companies who produced 5 to 10 stories for bi-weekly showings in cinemas between 1910 and 1979. They pre-date television which only became a household staple in the 1950s and early 1960s, and were the only way that millions of people worldwide could watch *moving* pictures of world and local news events. The cameramen, as the recently compiled database of newsreel content now reveals, were given assignment sheets and then went off to film the event, bringing material back and filling out their own post-shoot sheets with useful factual details and comments, plus delivering ephemera that might be of use to the commentators who wrote the scripts; this in the form of handouts or tickets or anything they deemed of use that they were given or found on location. So, they did the research for critical script needs such as the spelling of names and places. These cameramen were more than just technicians; they were the eyes and ears, thinking on the job about how best to capture the event and deliver the news. Of course in the early days they did not record sound. The style of the newsreel was to use a soundtrack and voiced commentary, with no natural sound, but often music instead. Their job, just like that of VJs, was made easier as technology developed and produced better designed and more lightweight cameras, cameras capable of recording sound as well. Tripods went from from being wooden and extremely heavy to becoming more portable when made of lightweight steel. Wooden tripods were used up until the 1970s. Lenses improved with zoom facilities and sound equipment was added too. A number of these changes came from the burgeoning movie industry in America where companies were developing new and better equipment all the time. They moved from the silent films of Charlie Chaplin that were shown in cinemas with a live piano accompaniment and dialogue boxes, to the talkies. As the popularity and relevance of newsreels died and the home-based TV set took over as a way of receiving and distributing or disseminating news, the newswire agencies filled the gap to supply film for TV, while the BBC and later the emergent independent or commercial TV stations in the UK began to send out their own news crews. If you watch the early news bulletins in the BBC archive, for example, you will see a male newsreader wearing a dinner jacket and bowtie, sitting at a desk and speaking to camera with an occasional still and even more occasional moving image. The assassination of J.F. Kennedy on 22 November 1963 was reported with only one still until some days later when film footage arrived from the US. In those days it was extremely expensive, £200 per minute of film, to send by trans-Atlantic cable. So it looked like picture radio.

Some programmes such as the BBC's ground-breaking 'Tonight', which started in 1957, got out into the field both at home and abroad using small hand-held clockwork cameras like the Bolex. This allowed the first nightly current affairs programme to report on events and stories in a different way. Reporter Trevor Philpot with cameraman Slim Hewitt managed to show the poverty and desperate living conditions of people living on the rubbish dumps of Lima, Peru by hiding the camera under his coat. This sounds familiar to much of present day covert filming – and it all came down to the portability of the camera.

A growing number of film directors in the feature film industry today use small cameras for special effects and sequences, putting them in cars for action shots, using them to give a fluidity of movement and that intimacy that the large, more sophisticated video or film cameras cannot provide.

So, moving towards a definition of videojournalism, let us hear from someone whose job it is to know:

> It is a production technique which offers a more distinctive, engaging, people-driven style of television. It involves the use of DV cameras ... but the technology is only part of the story. What is more important is the access and flexibility it offers, leading to our output having more original journalism. Also by equipping people with cameras and edit systems we open up a whole range of new possibilities. We are enabling people to tell their own stories rather than narrate them; we can film situations as they happen rather than stage them, and get to places we couldn't previously get to.
>
> (Lisa Lambden, Head of BBC SON&R Centre for Videojournalism)

Summary

Videojournalism combines journalism with video shooting.

However, questions remain. For example, was Dan Damon who worked as a reporter and cameraman but mainly used a professional-level camera a VJ? He thinks of himself as one because he worked alone. Working alone is part of the current definition of VJs who are in local TV, but in reality a good number of people work and have worked with someone else: a producer, fixers, translators or local print journalists. They research and help organise the filming. Few of those video pioneers I've interviewed for this book worked consistently alone, not in conflict zones or on difficult assignments; even with rebel forces there was someone to carry their tripod or help with their disguise and facilitate interviews or translate. However, they were usually the only person who used the camera and shot the footage. This might seem like a splitting of hairs, but in the telling of a part of history, it is important to detail exactly how the medium or production technique developed.

For some theorists, a further redefining is needed of those non-journalists who record video that is used by broadcasters for news and other programming or for the internet. This, it is argued, is *videography* practised by *videographers* (remember our fictitious scenario of the wave being recorded). The BBC terms those filming, not just for news but for features, documentary and entertainment programming too, 'self-op' shooters. When it recruited VJs ITN called them production journalists or PJs. The *Daily Telegraph* is looking to recruit videojournalists for its multi-media platform via the newspaper's website, and the newspaper group Johnston Press who own the *Yorkshire Post* amongst other papers has its journalists using video cameras and is also calling them videojournalists. The term is being used more because multi-media organisations need multi-skilled people who can record video too.

The following chapters will look at the history and development of videojournalism and video technology, setting it in social and political context. It will give practical advice from practising VJs, in local TV especially, and it will look to the new media use of video. Finally it will try to look ahead and see what the future might hold for video practitioners and those wanting to be part of the media.

Student questions

1   How did videojournalism come about?
2   Is it an alternative to professional newsgathering or do they co-exist?
3   Why is videojournalism particularly relevant today in the age of broadband internet and multi-media organisations?
4   Can anybody be described as a VJ?
5   Why is it difficult to define as a genre or medium of filmmaking?

2   The pre-video era

The social and political landscape in the UK when the first small video cameras were launched in the late 1980s affected the changes that then took place within broadcasting.

Politically it was the era of the 'Iron Lady' as the Soviet Union nicknamed the Prime Minister Margaret Thatcher. She was the UK's first woman in the top political job and told a conference of small businessmen and women that,

> I came to office with one deliberate intent: to change Britain from a dependent to a self-reliant society – from a give-it-to-me, to a do-it-yourself nation. A get-up-and-go, instead of a sit-back-and-wait-for-it Britain.

She could have been describing the do-it-yourself approach to videojournalism, picking up a camera and filming. Thatcher brought about radical reforms during her years in power under her particular brand of 'economic liberalism' that encouraged people to invest in the country's prosperity. She gave them the chance to buy their own homes by offering council housing for sale, sold off shares in the state utilities that were being privatised and encouraged private pension provision.

At the same time she confronted the trade unions whom she felt had too much power and were preventing change in the private and public sectors. The broadcast industry was deemed one of the worst culprits at holding employers to ransom. From their point of view, the unions felt they should see as big a slice of the 'pie' as possible, especially when ITV companies were making handsome profits from advertising. At this time the three broadcast union ABS, ACTT and BETA had around 60,000 members, compared to 25,000 in BECTU, the amalgamated union in 2007. The closed shop that operated in broadcasting ensured not only a certain level of pay but also standards within the industry. Getting your union card and being able to work was like the actors' union Equity still is today. You had to serve an apprenticeship, to have performed, directed, or worked at a number of projects, before you were allowed membership. So naturally the unions wanted to maintain the status quo. Qualified people ensured wage demands could be negotiated from a position of strength.

> There were all sorts of other restrictions relating to pay and hours of work called: double bubble, time and a half and the golden hour. The latter was a wonderful system where if you worked a shift without a ten hour break, you started on the rate of the day before so it kept multiplying – time and a half by time and a half. If you continued working for a whole week, you could be earning astronomic sums. The reason for this pay scale was that ITV initially drew its technical workforce from the film industry and imported film industry unions, and so adopted their pay scales, before thinking about how to get from old to the new, i.e. TV newsgathering. The film crews had 2 plus 2 plus 2: two on camera, two on sound, a clapper/loader (who held the clapper board to mark each take and also loaded and unloaded the film in the camera) and a lighting man. In 1982 the average earnings of cameramen was £55,000 per annum, a considerable wage by any industry standard. That was how good the ITV union system had been for technicians, so it was not surprising they were so defensive about it.
>
> (Mike Morris, former Head of Industrial Relations, ITN, now Head of HR at the South Bank)

The result of Thatcher's government policy was union strike action.

The BBC too was hit by strikes at the end of 1978 and into 1979. Its unions wanted their pay levels to come closer to those earned by their ITV counterparts (there was a 30 per cent discrepancy). In order to avoid a blackout over Christmas in 1978, BBC management agreed to a 15 per cent increase. The Corporation of course had the licence fee as its revenue, which was guaranteed so it was in a position to do this. Alan Sapper, General Secretary of the ACTT (the largest TV and film union), in 1978 when told about the damage the strikes were doing said, '£2 million of equipment lying unused? Good, that's a victory for us'. This reflected the union's attitude to new video equipment coming in that they saw as threatening and could mean large changes to the agreed working practices. Not content with their own pay, the ACTT pressed ITV companies for an increase of between 15–20 per cent in the summer of 1979. The companies refused and the result was a ten-week blackout of programmes – the longest in television history. Hit hard by an absence of advertising revenue, the ITV companies had to cave in and came up with a 22 per cent offer.

Industrial action was endemic in the UK; the TUC's (Trade Union Congress, which represents all the unions) role was to maintain and secure the best pay and working conditions for its members. The heads of the unions were household names: Jack Jones of the Transport and Genereal Workers Union, T&GWU; Joe Gormley of the National Miners' Union, NMU; Derek Robinson of the Car Workers' Union. They battled first with a Labour government and then with Margaret Thatcher from 1979 when she took office and in whom they met their match. The last show of the unions' strength was the 1984 miners' strike that lasted a year. It ended with the defeat of the miners and the government pressing ahead with legislative reforms which reduced the power of the unions for good. The closed shop was banned as were sympathy strikes. Members had to be balloted before action was called. It took the decision-making away from the union leaders and allowed members to vote individually, so that those who preferred to keep their jobs or not to strike could now have a say. How did this affect the broadcast companies? As Mike Morris remembers,

> In a general way, reform of union law, bringing an end to picketing and ballots for industrial action helped destroy ITV's monopoly position. It is easy to blame ITV management; I can remember being in management when staff could and did walk out. They just said at meetings, 'hands up for a strike' and off they walked. At least the advent of videotape meant you could run a TV station without technicians in early the 1980s, before the TVam dispute. Thames TV kept running without technical staff for weeks by just replaying programmes already recorded.

Mike Morris began his TV career at ITN.

> When I started in the 1960s it was an era when everything was on film. A journalist could cause a strike by touching a can of film. The technicians and union members' stance was that clear, 'we touch it, operate it, cut it and shoot it and you're in charge of words – end of story'. There was a clear demarcation between journalists and technicians. So the rise of videojournalism for me was defined primarily by radical changes in the industrial labour relations climate which took place in the 1970s, and changes in technology. It went from an era where there was this clear demarcation to a time where there is none, other than in highly specialised roles which might be defined as technical grades. Before as a journalist you wouldn't want to touch a can of film. It would unravel all over the floor, you wouldn't know how to handle it, hadn't been trained to do so. But a cassette was no problem, you could easily pick it up, stick it in a machine and press a button.

As ITN correspondent and VJ Sue Lloyd-Roberts found out, this small movement could threaten strike action too.

> I remember I had some footage on a VHS tape and walked into MCR (where the conversions and tape transfers were done) and there was a VCR machine and I slipped it into the machine and pressed play. There was almost a walk-out. Jobs were so demarcated. It was the 'oily rag' as

the cameraman and technicians were called (an ITN phrase) versus the journalist.

Morris explains how it then progressed, so that

once the technology changed, newsrooms and offices were full of these boxes of tapes, with journalists picking them up and technicians couldn't think of a reason why they shouldn't. For ITN and TV news there had to be concessions, we needed smaller crews. It was bitterly fought and strongly resisted but finally a news crewing agreement came into being. A news crew consisted of two plus one: sound, camera and lights when needed. It was regarded as radical by the unions. So when we got to the 1970s and there was the possibility of doing things with small cameras, super 8 [8mm film] and small clockwork cameras, still pre-video age, management went again to the unions to get permission to use them. We might ask, 'Can we give a clockwork camera to someone climbing Everest?' Their response was, 'we'll have to ask the shop', i.e. the union members. Then there would be another occasion of super 8 film of an event by an amateur where there couldn't possibly have been a professional crew and we'd ask again if we could use it. Small concessions were allowed by the unions, who let highly dubious material (in their opinion) past their professional stockade and effectively reduced their job security. ITN had people who at least realised that changes had to happen, that cameramen would one day operate sound and that journalists could and would operate technical equipment when and if needed.

In order to make this point clear I decided to make a video. So I sent a reporter to a TV station in Boston where they were already one-man-banding. A report was filmed showing an American journalist switching on their own lights, going filming on the road alone, or acting as a studio cameraperson. I was so worried about this getting out, that I divided the shot material in two and had two separate companies editing it using independent producers and then joined it together and showed it to staff at ITN, in the old Studio One in Wells Street. I did the presentation to a packed room and ran the video. Absolute silence.

ITN in 1988 had big negotiations called 'Into the 90s' with the unions, smoothing the way for multi-skilling. Looking for new obstacles to put in management's way, the unions at all the TV stations made technical quality an issue instead.

TVam, the commercial breakfast news channel that began in 1984, was seen as the company who put the full stop on the broadcast unions' power. When it won the licence, TVam employed a number of highly-paid presenters to attract viewers. However, the station built up losses of £20 million within three years and so in order to cut costs, its tough Australian managing director Bruce Gyngell confronted the unions with his plans. These involved installing automated studios and reducing staff numbers. The ensuing strike ran for months, with Gyngell eventually winning out, and replacing unionised staff with untrained, non-members. While neither the station nor Gyngell survived beyond 1992 and the new round of franchise sales for ITV, he had set a precedent for tackling the unions head on. Thatcher sent Gyngell a personal letter of commiseration because she admired his tactics. In fact he won a Department of Industry Award for innovations in staff development!

While reducing the power of the unions was one thing, Thatcher had yet to implement her plans for radically changing the face of the broadcasting industry. These were outlined in the 1988 White Paper and proposed more competition for commercial television and an allowance for the early use of two extra channels from the BSB (government) satellites.

The first satellite, Telstar, was launched in 1962 allowing live viewing of the Olympic Games in Tokyo in 1964 on UK TV screens. The White Paper also suggested a new method of funding the BBC by subscription (something that is still on the agenda today).

In a show of independence and defiance at the government threats, the BBC in November 1988 screened a Panorama documentary called 'Death on the Rock'. It investigated the murder of three alleged IRA terrorists by British army assassins in Gibraltar, linking it to the government's controversial 'shoot to kill' policy in Northern Ireland. The Conservative government retaliated by curbing the BBC's independence in new terms under the Broadcasting Act of 1990. This was based on the Peacock Report that saw 'free markets and consumer choice' as the guiding principles of the government's broadcasting policy. So the Act tightened its grip on the BBC but relaxed regulation in ITV and allowed for greater competition.

The Broadcasting Act 1990 brought several changes to the ITV network, which was officially renamed Channel 3. The franchises were awarded on a 'highest-bidder' basis rather than the previous 'beauty contest', i.e. where the station's achievements were looked at. The Independent Broadcast Authority was abolished, and replaced by the Independent Television Commission (ITC). The 1993 auction saw big changes. Westcountry Television won the South West England franchise, replacing TVSW. Meridian Broadcasting won the South and South-East England franchise, replacing TVS. Carlton Television won the London weekday franchise, replacing Thames Television. Sunrise Television (soon renamed GMTV) won the Breakfast franchise, replacing TVam. Teletext Ltd won the National Teletext franchise, replacing ORACLE. The 1993 franchise round was followed by consolidation where most of the companies continued merging until only one company remained. Granada bought LWT and Yorkshire-Tyne Tees Television (which had merged in 1993), Carlton Communications bought Central and Westcountry; MAI/UNM bought Meridian Broadcasting, Anglia Television and HTV; Scottish Media Group bought Grampian Television.

In 2000, Granada bought Meridian, Anglia and HTV from UNM, but had to sell HTV to Carlton. In 2001, Granada bought Border. Granada and Carlton then owned all the franchises for England and Wales. In February 2004, Granada Media and Carlton Communications were finally allowed to merge, to form one single company: ITV plc. It owns six additional television channels (five using the ITV brand), broadcasting on cable, satellite and digital terrestrial: ITV2, ITV3, ITV4, ITV Play, CITV Channel and Men and Motors. The company also has interests in cinema advertising businesses, the Irish television channel TV3 and ITN. In 2005, the company bought the website Friends Reunited. Channel Four was allowed to sell its own advertising time in competition with ITV. Thatcher also showed her 'fondness' for Rupert Murdoch by allowing him to set up sky television and then take over its *publicly-owned* competitor BSB (British Satellite Broadcasting). When BSB went to Downing Street to complain to Thatcher about Sky, she told them to 'stop whining'. So Murdoch slipped under the net, making his acquisition just before the IBA was replaced by the new ITC – Independent Television Commission. He might not have been able to accomplish his coup with their stricter guidelines.

The birth of the satellite age had begun with BSkyB, accompanied by a cable revolution too. The Broadcasting Act was radical in leaving these two new types of broadcasting open to the free-market forces and unhampered by legislation. Developments in fibre optic technology allowed for the idea that a new 'wired society' could become a reality, with the telephone wires able to carry much more information, bringing with it television programme services too. Following the US where there was a proliferation of TV channels via cable, the UK dipped its foot into the cable option, but it never really succeeded in attracting sufficient investment.

Satellite gained ground rapidly from 1989, helped by the fact that BSkyB, transmitting on the Astra satellite, was not subject to public service broadcasting requirements. It also opted for broadcasting in PAL, not the government-prescribed MAC encoded system and this allowed for subscribers to just pay for a dish and set-up box, rather than new TV receivers. Murdoch of course did not have to deal with the unions either; he set his own terms of employment, he introduced 12-hour shifts, for example, and his pay levels were lower than ITV or the BBC, but he still recruited staff. As BSkyB grew, so did the cable industry, with its agreement to relay the Murdoch channels giving it some extra puff. Cable was never, however, going to match the explosion in satellite broadcasting.

The same year that the Broadcast Act came in, Thatcher was out of office, her historic third term coming to an abrupt end. Her leadership was challenged over her refusal to countenance European integration, leaving her no option but to step down and see John Major take over as Prime Minister. The changes she had wrought in the broadcasting industry over her eleven years in power, changed it for good. Moreover the 'information superhighway' that the then US Vice President Al Gore described in the early

1990s was about to overtake everything. Digital technology, he said, would provide:

> a network of networks, transmitting messages and images at the speed of light across every continent [which would] bring economic progress, strong democracies, better environmental management, improved health care and a greater sense of shared stewardship of our small planet.

His vision of the internet was not yet happening, but technology was changing very fast, including the development of video technology too. The other great changes about to take place were in the political landscape of Eastern Europe and Russia. Just before Thatcher's departure, Soviet leader Mikhail Gorbachev set about trying to bring in radical reforms, but the world's eyes moved from the USSR to Eastern Europe where momentous events were taking place: 1989 was the year of revolutions, when the Communist regimes fell like dominos knocking each other over. The Velvet Revolution in Poland in September was followed by the Hungarian on 23 October followed by the Berlin Wall falling between Communist East Germany and West Berlin on 9 November. This in turn the next day led to the fall of Todor Zhivkov, Communist dictator in Bulgaria, to the disintegration of Czechoslovakia on 28 November and to the Romanian Revolution in December. The formal end of the Cold War between the Soviet Union and the US was signed in Malta on 3 December. It was such a rapidly changing European political scene that made it hard for television news to keep up with its coverage and reports.

The last of the old-style Communist leaders was Nicolae Ceausescu of Romania. On the morning of 21 December, Ceausescu addressed a mass assembly of a 100,000 people to condemn the previous week's protest and demonstrations in the town of Timişoara. As he was addressing the crowd from the balcony of the Central Committee building, sudden movement coming from the outskirts of the mass assembly and the sound of what various sources have reported as fireworks, bombs, or guns incensed the crowd who thought they were being fired upon. Anger turned into action and one of the first buildings to be taken by the crowds and revolutionaries was the TV station in one of the fiercest battles with the army. All of this was filmed by Frontline VJs and others who found themselves in a classic revolutionary struggle. A firing squad executed Ceausescu and his wife Elena.

These revolutions were propelled by young people's frustrations; they were the ones protesting in the streets when their parents had long given up on the struggle for freedom. TV played a central part by beaming pictures via illegal satellites of Western pop culture. I remember watching young people watching pop videos of singers on yachts, wearing fashionable clothes and dancing or prancing in luxury settings. It seemed so alluring when sitting in the grey concrete wastes of the Communist countries. Everyone in the videos seemed to be having so much fun, when the bread queues, empty shops and poor choice in clothes or music was their everyday reality. VJs like me followed the trail of unfolding events and watched people reach out for democracy, capitalism and the dreams of Coca-Cola, blue jeans and whatever else the people of those countries thought a 'free' world could offer. Before independence, any traveller was offered ludicrous sums for their Levis on the street, and many (including myself) happily exchanged them for dollars, the new unofficial currency of the black market that rapidly developed in sought-after Western goods. Immediately after independence the Eastern European countries were awash in blue denim, imported and copied after Western styles. It was a sign of the times, that finally their wishes had come true.

Margaret Thatcher got on well with the architect of the end of Communism, Soviet President Mikhail Gorbachev. His changes proved her theories that collectivist solutions did not work, and that capitalism and market forces were the only answer. She welcomed the freeing of the republic nations under his policy of 'perestroika'. These reforms introduced in June 1987 were to restructure the Soviet economy. They also helped contribute to its decline and the eventual disintegration of the Soviet Union in 1991. Gorbachev's measures, especially to do with foreign trade and ownership, were bold and in this period of 'glasnost' opened the country to investors. The Soviet Ministry of Foreign Trade's monopoly on most trade operations was broken. Decentralisation allowed for regional and local organisations and individual state enterprises to conduct foreign trade. The most significant of Gorbachev's reforms in the foreign economic sector allowed foreigners to invest in the Soviet Union in the form of joint ventures with Soviet ministries, state enterprises, and cooperatives. The economic changes did not do much to restart the country's economy, it was too far gone, and in fact the reverse happened and it went into a tailspin. Hyper-inflation, a spiralling rouble currency and a worsening of living conditions resulted in an attempted coup d'état on 19 August 1991. It failed through lack of support both from the individual republics and from the outside world. Nevertheless the lack of confidence was apparent and this brought down the government. Gorbachev resigned and the threads holding the individual states together snapped.

Why is it important to re-tell these dramatic events of 1989? The answer is that the same year saw the arrival of the age of the Hi8 camera, together with a number of individual journalists and others intent on using the small dv cameras to record events and to earn a living from it. Frontline News was, as detailed in the following chapter, set up in a Bucharest hotel in the midst of the Romanian Revolution. Insight News was also established, harnessing a new technology to capture on tape an emerging new world order. As described in the next chapter on pioneers, early VJs shot and sold footage and reports from the crisis torn regions to news editors worldwide. Of course they had their own news crews in the regions, but they could only cover a small part of what was happening. The material documented the revolutions, demonstrations, fighting and lives of people in turmoil across Eastern Europe, and then as it spread in 1990 to the Baltic States with Lithuania followed by Estonia and Latvia, to the Russian Republics, to Yugoslavia in 1991 and Albania in 1992. No one had ever seen pictures like these before and what news editor would refuse exclusive footage? After all they did not have to pay travel expenses, nor insure the freelancers, nor worry about them while out in hostile situations. The risk and the brunt of the cost in time above all was borne by the filmmakers themselves. The irony is that the unions had been there to prevent exploitation of members and yet here were those same members pushing for the acceptance of a new way of working that was both exploitative and badly paid. Nick Guthrie remembers how:

> I supported VJs because they provided programmes with reports from places that others wouldn't go to. The VJs were freelancers who specialised in original ideas, and I wasn't into taking them away and giving them to staff to do. We had the budget for it, decent budgets then. I was Foreign Editor on BBC's *Newsnight* programme and I bought ten Handycams and handed them out. I gave them to producers and correspondents so we got a different source of material from that provided by professional crews. It made the journalists more visually aware of what they were trying to report and also gave them an insight into how hard it was to get the right pictures.

Ron McCullagh, who was one of those VJs employed by Guthrie on BBC Breakfast News, who went on to start Insight News, remembers slightly differently how it was in those early days:

> We were called the 'fucking indies', lower than pond life. I had been a respected journalist in the BBC until I started doing this. I took on the mantle of irresponsibility, along with others who were some of the most courageous humanitarian-minded journalists of the time. But they represented such a threat to the industry. News programmes ran on straightforward principles: you employed staff to make programmes and then there were the agencies too. So it got difficult when someone phoned up and said 'I've got great material'. It was a pain; you had to give them money. 'We just don't do this', they'd say, because we'd presented them with a problem for their budgets and balance sheets. They didn't find it easy to adapt to VJs and freelancers.

In 1991 the BBC World Service TV also issued small video cameras to correspondents and they were trained in how to operate cameras and edit. In 1994 BBC World evolved from World Service TV and its first editor, Rick Thompson, remembers how he:

> inherited a Hi8 system where a lot of overseas stringers had been issued with cameras and had some rudimentary training. We pushed this as far

as it would go at the time and it definitely helped BBC World to provide a range of features unmatched by CNN.

To this day BBC World continues to use VJs and reports from stringers and correspondents (some based in the UK too). It set up a special features desk for commissioning, nurturing and delivering five two-and-a-half minute features per day to run on BBC World TV news programmes. This has now been cut back.

ITN began to recruit VJs in 1998. They were driven by necessity as ITN had no newsgathering teams outside London. The new Channel 5 lunchtime bulletin was to be broadcast at midday, ahead of ITN's 12.30 bulletin, so news footage was needed. You had to have those court arrivals and stories covered and the cheapest way was to have a number of VJs. So on 2 January 1998 ITN had four in place in Liverpool, Bristol, Tamworth and Edinburgh. Three had previously been working at the cable Channel One. Their brief was to report to the core news desk in London. Their numbers increased to 12 but the scheme only lasted two years and was closed when the new ITV deal allowed the regional companies, Yorkshire, Tyne Tees and Granada, to get their material elsewhere, not just from ITN. Giles Croot, who was the news editor for the core news desk and looked after the VJs, explains how it worked:

> I liaised with the ITN channels 3, 4, 5, IRN radio (owned by ITN) and online, and my job was to decide what needed to be done as stories by the VJs. The main stories had to be covered, stories that the channel would like from the VJ regions were next, followed by the wish list of stories that could be done anywhere in the country. We started with the Sony VX1000 cameras and then upgraded to the Canon XL1 that we thought was better quality. The VX was not reliable enough. We adapted the cameras with sound boxes (like the Beech box), gave them proper mics and lighting kits. The people we used were journalists who had then got to learn camera skills. Lots of pictures were wobbly at the start. The exception was in Northern Ireland where we employed Terry Agar who had been a despatch rider and then became a cameraman. We used him as a VJ because you had to have someone who was streetwise and he had good contacts. VJs sent in rushes, just raw footage, without commentaries, or pieces to camera. Occasionally they did voice stories for radio, but they were there to send pictures with interviews for the main bulletins. They were on call 7am–7pm, five days a week, sometimes weekends too. There were lots of issues about how they were deployed and if it was a lousy job, people at ITN would say 'get a VJ to do it', instead of a cameraman. They fed their material from the ITV regional newsrooms where there were lines direct to ITN. They also could use the OB [outside broadcast] trucks, of which we had about eight out and about to send us material. Or, they could go to any nearby racecourse

and use the SIS [satellite] links there. These were for transmitting horse races 'live' and linked to ITN in London.

We landed up with VJs in Bristol, Newbury, Maidstone, Birmingham, Nottingham, Manchester, Leeds, Newcastle and Edinburgh. Having VJs meant no 'TVam moments'. This was when the breakfast station was covering the Conservative party conference in 1984 when an IRA 100lb bomb went off in Brighton. The blast tore apart the Grand Hotel where members of the Cabinet were staying. Prime Minister Margaret Thatcher and her husband Dennis narrowly escaped injury. TVam had no camera crew there and went on air without pictures. The then regulatory body, the IBA, threatened to pull their broadcast licence. Among the injured were Trade and Industry Secretary Norman Tebbit, his wife Margaret and Government Chief Whip, John Wakeham. Five people were killed including Conservative MP Sir Anthony Berry, and John Wakeham's first wife Roberta. We had to make sure we were covered nationwide.

Croot has examples of where VJ filming made a difference to the ITN coverage of news: when Hillary Clinton was on a visit in the UK, Terry Agar was in the crowd on the other side of road from the news crews and got her coming right up to him to talk to the crowds. So different, more intimate shots were incorporated into the news report. Also when the fighter bombers left the UK for Kosovo, ITN could afford to keep a VJ at the airfield waiting for two days. So they broke the story with the first pictures. A local story of a seven-year-old who could do a hole in one on his local golf course was got onto News at Ten that night as the 'and finally' slot for amusing, touching end pieces.

Looking back, Giles Croot says,

> using VJs in this way needed a lot of looking after. They never came into the edit suites, never saw how their rushes were used and were out there by themselves. If we had continued using them I think the idea was to have around 20 who could if need be pair up with each other on occasion too.

The first widespread use of the Hi8 camera in features as opposed to news came in 1993 with the BBC programme called Video Nation. It showed 'video diaries' shot by non-journalists over one year where they filmed their everyday lives. This could be seen as the birth of the citizen journalist, for the Community Programme Unit distributed a number of cameras across the UK to ordinary people. It became immensely popular and more than 10,000 tapes were shot and sent in to the BBC who edited and showed around 1,300 of them. The first one was called Mirror by Gordon Hencher. Viewing figures were between 1 and 9 million. This success was described in *The Guardian* 'the immediacy of these programmes is entirely different to anything shot by a crew. There seems to be nothing between you, not even the glass' (by which they no doubt meant the TV screen).

Video Nation continues to the present day and is part of the BBC English Regions New Media output. The films can now be seen on the BBC 'Where I live' sites online, and the format of handing cameras to people continues.

Looking back to a pre-video newsgathering age, it was a period of great social change in ways of working. The end of the broadcast unions' power allowed the first video cameras to come in, and eventually for the VJ to begin to operate them. Over two decades later, the industry is still being driven by technological change.

> We lived through the heroic age of TV news, we were pioneers doing things not done before, but we didn't realise it then. The excitement has gone now. Before you either worked for ITN or BBC, they were the only news games in town. Now there is a plethora of opportunities in what you can do, but now as an observer I can see the development of media is exponential whether podcasting or mobile phone casting or local TV, as technology and bandwidth changes. I have no idea though where it's going to lead.
>
> (Mike Morris}

One man with an idea of the future is Vin Ray, who says that for him,

> videojournalism is definitely still evolving in two ways, as a craft in the way people do it and culturally in terms of its acceptance inside the organisation. There has been opposition to videojournalism amongst the staff because people feel it's lowering craft standards, and is threatening to those who haven't done camera and editing and might be expected to do it. It gives you something more, BBC stuff looks so overproduced sometimes, so the BBC has recognised this is not just cost effective but a stylistic matter too. When Foreign Editor at News, I remember some guy coming in saying, 'I'm going to Groszny [in Chechnya] will you pay for me to go there?' I replied with the words of all foreign editors down the years, 'If you get anything good give us a ring'. I wouldn't do that these days because he was in the parliament building when it got stormed. It was fabulous rough and raw footage, and you felt right in the middle of it. But he was alone, no flak jacket, with nothing more than a monumental amount of chutzpah. We probably fleeced him on what we paid him. He got stuff we wouldn't be prepared to risk our staff to get and that raises moral issues today.

Of course the BBC ran the footage nonetheless because of its exclusive nature and that, as we'll see in the next chapter is how VJs managed to keep going, paid for their courageous, maybe foolhardy, methods of newsgathering. None of this was possible without the technology and what follows is the story of just how those Hi8 cameras came to be produced.

How electronic newsgathering equipment came to market

It is a story very much dominated by Sony, the leading manufacturer and one who had a philosophy and style of working; as you'll read, it sounds a bit like a science fiction film script with the scientists pushing forward for newer and ever better inventions. Back in 1962 new technology and machines were spoken of as pure conjecture. 'Gorblimey' miracles are what Donald Edwards, speaking at a BBC lunch-time lecture, called them. 'There might', he said, 'be a transistorised video tape in colour [everything was still shot in black and white] for camera people to use and an electronic typewriter that may show words on a screen'.

The personal computer was also still some two decades away. Even when it arrived it sounded like a sci-fi machine. In 1981 PCW (PC World) wrote a world exclusive review of the very first IBM PC, the Model 5150's launch, which took place at a press conference in New York on 12 August 1981.

> With more than a little help from its friends, IBM has come up with a real stunner. The system has much to commend it, both for serious and fun applications, since it can grow from a fairly expensive cassette-based configuration to a full-blown twin disk/colour graphics machine. The public is becoming aware of the usefulness of these machines and prices are dropping. Microsoft, for example, was involved right from the beginning. However, at the moment the machine is only sold in the US. IBM will not say when, if ever, it will come to Britain. The minimum configuration is in two parts: a system unit, which houses the memory, processor, loudspeaker, power supply and slots for up to five expansion cards; and a keyboard, connected by a six-foot coiled flex. A monitor or domestic television is also needed and, for those without disks, a domestic tape recorder with a DIN connection. IBM supplies an Epson printer as its standard listing device, although you can attach a printer of your own choosing.
>
> (http://www/pcworld.com/article/126671-1/article.html)

We're jumping back another two decades, to the early 1960s, when the Sony factory and design studios in Japan were working to produce a video tape recorder. This would eventually lead to a home market video camera too. However, it all began with the CV2000 that in 1964 was marketed as the world's first home-use video recorder. It was a reel-to-reel recorder and the picture quality was so good (in black and white) that it was used by institutions, hospitals and schools as well as for home use. The Sony team behind this effort was led by Nobutoshi Kihara. His boss was Masaru Ibuka, a man of reputed vision who said upon widespread admiration at the quality of the video machine, 'technology does not abide by common sense. Our goal is to break down ideas people have come to accept as common sense'.

Interestingly a story about the early days of audio recording in Sony shows exactly the opposite, how a sensible stab at development proved correct. After the war Sony were apparently trying to copy US and German audio tape recorders. They had to make the tape by hand, using paper cut in strips. At first they could not get it to work by mixing iron filings with glue and painting it on the paper. After a while they realised that the iron filings were too strong (magnetically) to be influenced by the record head; so nothing was recorded and nothing replayed. After trial and error they found that ferric oxide was easier to record with a weak magnetic field from the record head. However, what they didn't realise was that this first attempt was a form of metal particle tape which has become the standard today. They had invented it before, didn't know it and then abandoned it only to re-invent it decades later when new technology could make it work.

Returning to the official Sony history, their new video tape machine was soon found wanting and the sales people requested colour models and asked engineers if they could design a VCR that used a cassette tape similar to an audio tape recorder. The story goes of how Kihara grumbled,

> the construction of a VCR is very complex. It will be extremely difficult to build a machine that will use a cassette tape, let alone in colour. You don't understand what you are asking the engineers to do!

Nevertheless, his boss Ibuka persisted, saying,

> look how easily audio tape recorders can be used thanks to the cassette tape! Why can't we incorporate this function into video players? This is the obvious next step that has to be taken in the development of this product.

Deep down, Kihara knew that Ibuka was right. And so it came to pass that a VCR able to play a tape housed in a cassette and that had an automatic loading function too was produced in 1968 – after many failed attempts. 'So you've managed to build this marvellous machine. Just think, the next one will be even better!' Ibuka said when he was shown the first prototype U-matic machine. Ibuka was tireless in the pursuit of his dreams and constantly set demanding targets for his engineers. 'It can't be done', were words that he would not easily accept. 'I love seeing Ibuka-san with a smile on his face, so I always do my best', said Kihara, referring to the obvious delight with which Ibuka greeted any new product or technology. No sooner had the prototype U-matic been completed in 1969, then Ibuka directed Kihara to commence work on the development of a next-generation video tape recorder. Smaller was always better, so a cassette tape the size of the Sony Business Diary, identical to a Japanese paperback book size, was required. To put this research and development in a historic context, remember that at this time, in the United States, President John F. Kennedy was urging the scientific community to get a man on the moon. Speaking about the prospect of sending astronauts to the moon in 1961, Kennedy said 'No single space project in this period will be more impressive to mankind, or more important for the long-range exploration of space. And none will be so difficult or expensive to accomplish'.

The space race was against the Soviet Union; both countries wanted to win to prove their scientific superiority and to show their military strength. America came up trumps on 20 July 1969 when Neil Armstrong landed on the moon.

Sony came up with its small book-sized machine in 1973. The following year a visit by Joseph Flaherty, then vice president at CBS, one of the three major US television networks, was instrumental in changing newsgathering for ever. He had come to ask if Sony could develop a U-matic model specifically for commercial broadcasting. Flaherty wanted a product that could produce the same image quality as 16mm film, but that was lighter and easier to use than existing models. Producing news reports with a film camera offered far greater mobility than with a video system, which at that time required a huge van equipped with a studio camera and recorder called a VTR. Flaherty said 'the ideal system would incorporate the advantages of both 16mm cameras and video'. CBS years earlier had combined the industrial-use U-matic system with an industrial-use hand-held video camera to achieve both the mobility of 16mm cameras and the real-time image processing capabilities of video. Thanks to the revolutionary U-matic video system, it was able to deliver images from President Nixon's visit to Moscow in 1974 faster than its competitors. However, as the U-matic had originally been developed as a home-use system, many specifications still needed to be improved to make it suitable for broadcast-use, hence the visit by Flaherty. At this time, however, the Sony director of the Video Division, Morizono, had no intention of entering the broadcast market. Impressed by Flaherty's persistence he agreed to take on the project. He called Masayuki Takano and other engineers into his office and, in the presence of Flaherty, said, 'I have decided to cooperate with Flaherty of CBS to make a broadcast standard U-matic system. I want you to develop a product in one year'. The usual time allotted for product development at Sony was two years, but by 1976, a broadcast-use U-matic system, the Broadcasting Video (BV) series, became a reality. The system incorporated shooting, recording, and editing functions in its compact, high-quality body and heralded a new method of news reporting dubbed ENG (electronic news gathering) by Morizono and Flaherty. By introducing ENG, broadcast stations were able to drastically cut costs, and in a short time broadcast stations worldwide began converting to the Sony system. The system's potential did not end with news gathering. Subsequently, the system was adopted for application in the area of EFP (electronic field programming) as well.

The development of the small video camera

While the video recorder was being developed, a revolution was going on in camera design too. The release of the CCD-V8 or Video8 as it was known for the consumer market, meant the prevailing VHS camera and SVHS or super VHS was being challenged. JVC responded by developing the C-cassette. Based on the VHS standard, the C-cassette was approximately one-quarter the size of a VHS cassette tape. JVC then released the VHS-C camcorder. Sony set to work to make the Sony camcorder even smaller and lighter. Development expenses mounted over a three-year period, and the product became unprofitable. Sony then literally went back to the drawing board and held an in-house competition among designers to create the 'most desirable' 8mm camcorder. Many useable designs were submitted, and Sony used them as a starting point for Project 88, which started at the end of 1986. The new project team's target was to create a camcorder by 8 August 1988. It wanted to create a model small enough to be used with one hand while keeping the picture and sound quality. With the sound they found that if a highly sensitive hi-fi microphone was built into the body of the camcorder, it would pick up the noise made by the unit's other parts. The solution was to use two microphones, one to nullify the internal noise and the other to record sound. A new and smaller 6X zoom lens was designed, but reducing the size of the lens meant the F number which determines the amount of light that enters the lens became lower, resulting in a darker image. The answer was to double the light sensitivity of the CCD. As John Ive, a former Sony employee and now an independent technology solutions expert recalls,

> 8mm established Sony as the market leader for consumer camcorders and were a great success – others adopted the format and VHS was squeezed out of the consumer camcorder business. We will not know how many were used professionally as they are bought through the same channel as consumer and not counted separately but we know broadcasters used them extensively through discussions. After 8mm, dv followed and Sony's success grew further.

Sequentially, the Video8 camera developed into Super8, then Hi8. The Sony V5000 and 6000 cameras followed but they were larger and heavier with useful audio meters and also could be shoulder-mounted. I owned a V5000 and its appearance gave you more authority, you looked more like a 'real' TV journalist, whereas the Hi8 looked unconvincing. However, travelling with it and concealing it in difficult filming situations was a lot harder. So when the next generation of cameras appeared like the Sony VX1000 and the Panasonic EZ1, they were taken up by VJs and broadcasters in the early 1990s as the first plausible alternative to the professional cameras. As Andy Benjamin, at DV Solutions, the BBC's in-house video department, recalls,

Illustration 2.1 ITV VJs in action, Bristol Balloon Fiesta, 2000

the VX1000 was the first light-weight quality digital video camera so that was the real revolution. You could get broadcast quality in a package that cost a tenth of the existing equipment. The size meant you could be very responsive. You could even afford to own a camera. So if you were doing an 'obsdoc' [observational documentary] and something happened at 3am you could get out and film it. If you didn't have a camera you'd either have missed the shots or else had to pay a fortune to have a crew on 24 hour standby. I remember the first time I saw digital video was at the trade show in Amsterdam in 1995. It was a Panasonic EZ1, and you couldn't alter the sound levels. The Sony VX1000 had manual to override automatic settings for sound which made it better. In fact we still had to try various adaptations to improve sound and then Beech box came from Beech Electronics in America who produced it. It made the camera a bit heavier but it worked.

Before that had been a whole range of Hi8 semi-professional versions but the main problem was picture quality. It was grainy and the flickering band at the bottom of the picture made it technically unacceptable for broadcast and not allowed except in exceptional cases. Dv made all the difference.

Documentary-maker Chris Terril shot a series called Soho Stories on the VX1000, which was a 'fly on the wall' observational series, where he spent a year based in London's Soho district in the West End, following various characters. It was transmitted at 11pm on BBC2 in 1995 and is remembered for portraying a unique closeness to and intimacy with the people. It was ground-breaking filmmaking and all down to the new dv camera. In fact the VX1000 was not renowned for its quality, the PD100 which was the first with flip-out screen and a palm-corder followed. It weighed 900gm which was less than a kilo. It was the ideal size, many felt, as you could hold it steady in your hand and still press the buttons.The VX2000 series was then marketed and that was followed by the PD150 and 170 plus the ZX1 which is now seen as well suited to the needs of VJs. In fact Sony recently brought out the V1 as a lightweight version of the Z1. This is because at 2.2 kilos the Z1 is heavy to hand-hold and the BBC technical training department for instance is now seeing people with wrist injuries and joint problems. If you put a wide angle lens on front the weight is almost 3 kilos. So while picture and sound quality have improved, the concept of a lightweight small camera has somewhere been lost. Newer still are the HD and tapeless models. Videojournalists embrace each new model but joke that 'Sony always builds in a design fault so that the next model has to be bought'. Not true, says Ive,

> it happens by default for consumer-derivative products. Professionals would of course find things they didn't like or missing functionality in the consumer derivative products – often not there because they were not important for consumer use. Also because the Sony consumer group did most of the design they rarely reworked existing models but assigned changes to the next model. So complaints were often not incorporated on the basis that it was not viable to rework such a low cost product. At the top end professional level it was quite normal to have a revised model as new features were added or problems fixed.

Sony features in this section so prominently because it became the benchmark and brand for professional broadcasters, even though JVC, Panasonic and Canon matched them in the consumer market. The competition helped spur on newer and better models, always aiming at smaller, more compact and easy to use. The consumer, whether professional or just from the domestic market, is the driver and as you'll see in Chapter 8, the BBC is now working with Panasonic on what they see as their perfect camcorder, putting their demands first. The technology has not stopped evolving and it is now like the chicken and the egg seeing which comes first: will it be what the consumer wants for the new multi-media world of communications, or will it be what is offered by the manufacturers?

Student questions

1   How did the broadcast industry change?
2   Would the new video technology have been allowed in if the unions had retained their power?

3   What momentous events were VJs able to record and sell to the broadcasters?
4   How did VJs become more established as news providers?
5   Did economics play a role in videojournalism being taken seriously?

3 Videojournalist pioneers

While the history of television news has been well documented, there is a part of it that has not been recorded. That is from 1987 and the rise of videojournalists. So this chapter tells the story of some of those early pioneers. They include me. We were all ready and willing to try out something new, to pick up cameras and 'have a go'. As you have read in the previous chapter, the timing was right, events were happening that needed covering, the cameras and the technology were there and so were the people.

Videojournalism was at this time a medium that challenged the traditional way that TV news had been produced and the agreed industry-set standards of picture and sound quality that were acceptable for broadcast. Material was checked before it went out by the technicians for its quality. Material not shot by union members was not permitted for broadcast. That was how a closed shop operated and the unions protected the rights of their members. As the previous chapter touched on, the unions' walls were breached and each exception went to appeal for broadcast. As reports and material were let through, the gap widened. Then there was a flood, helped by legislation ending union control. No one hankered for the past where film got scratches on it and cameras had hairs stuck in the 'gate' through which the film ran that showed up during edits and ruined reports, and where sound was not nearly as good. So while everyone agreed that the electronic age improved the speed of delivery, the early video pictures and sound quality of the small video cameras left a lot to be desired. It was inevitable that the Hi8 camera footage was not up to professional standards as the cameras were for consumers. Moreover, many of us who first picked them up were not trained in camerawork nor sound or lighting techniques. So the Hi8 cameras got nicknames like 'sillycam' by Martin Bell (former BBC correspondent), 'willycam' in honour of those testosterone-charged operators, 'wobbly scope' commenting on the quality of material, and the 'toilet camera' by Dan Damon because as he said, 'you could go into a toilet, turn off the light and still record'.

The first videojournalist is not easy to pinpoint. Everyone who picked up a camera during the late 1980s believes they were 'first'. They all deserve recognition for their work. Some were not journalists, nor used Hi8 cameras, nor worked alone, nor edited their own material. For example, Channel One staff were labelled VJs even though they used the large professional cameras. In any period of experimentation all sorts of people are attracted to new ways of working, new technology and want to test it or try it out or use it as an opportunity for making money, furthering their careers, changing their lives or just shaking the establishment tree.

Did any of these pioneers have any common characteristics? I would say that they shared a liking for adventure, for doing something different, difficult and challenging. Some were reckless, some got killed in action and others distinguished themselves in highlighting conflicts and events that otherwise would have gone unreported in the world. The risk-taking and independent filming goes on today. The conflict in Iraq has had the highest ever number of journalists, camerapeople and media staff killed. According to the International Federation of Journalists in 2006, 155 journalists were murdered, 68 of them in Iraq. Most of the first modern-day videojournalism work was done abroad. Why? Well as discussed in Chapter 2, the small lightweight video cameras came out at the same time as a number of events were taking place. To recap: political events in the Soviet Union and Eastern Bloc countries meant there was an increasing number of conflicts and stories breaking which were impossible to cover, even using traditional crewing, because of the costs involved. So freelance journalists prepared to enter countries covertly with Hi8 cameras, while posing as tourists or in some way avoiding detection, and were in some ways encouraged by foreign news editors. They would utter the immortal lines, 'I can't commission you, of course, but if you come back with something, let me know'. The technology helped; the small mini dv cassettes could easily be hidden or passed off as music cassettes and the cameras did not look threatening. The broadcast trade unions 'closed shop' was being challenged around this time as companies sought to cut their costs, so the timing was good. News editors and management were prepared at this point to push Hi8 footage for broadcast.

Why did these first VJs do it? Well why do people climb mountains? The answer is to see if they can. I would argue that many countries were closed at that time, in the late 1980s and little footage or material had come out of them. No one really knew what Albania looked like under Enver Hoxha, nor Romania, nor the far-flung parts of the Soviet Union especially Central Asia. Similarly in Africa and South East Asia, while the main news stories were being covered, a great many were not, because of the logistics and costs of getting there and back. Remember cheap air travel had yet to come in and fares were two or three times what they are today. Travel to many regions was dangerous and broadcasters were not prepared to risk their staff's lives, or to let them spend weeks covering a story. So the opportunity was there for those intrepid and even foolish enough to follow in the footsteps of Victorian adventurers or those newspaper men who covered the Crimean War, or the fictitious Boot in Evelyn Waugh's *Scoop*. The results, re-examined two decades later, show some remarkable and unique video material, often telling devastating and eye-opening tales of conflict, injustice, human rights abuse and the desperation of people's lives. Slavery in Burma, the Chinese occupation of Tibet, the battle of the Kurds for their rights, the secret concentration camps in China, the selling of human parts, the Romanian orphans left to die, child labour, sex trafficking and countless genocides, famines and civil wars, in Africa especially.

The rest of this chapter tells the stories of a few of those pioneers who began the modern history of videojournalism. It is *not* a definitive list, but gives a flavour of their work, how they worked and what videojournalism meant to them. Each story is divided into sections detailing their journalistic status, travels and reports and also camera or filming techniques and tips.

Nick Downey

Status

An ex-SAS soldier, Nick Downey had seen action in the Rhodesian War of Independence in the 1970s. There he had met with a number of cameramen and crews working for ITN, BBC and APTN. He had watched how they worked and decided to try it himself. The crews at the time were three people: cameraman, sound recordist and reporter. However, some of the agency cameramen did work without reporters and sometimes without a sound recordist. One Rhodesian-based (now Zimbabwe) cameraman actually had his dog listed as the sound recordist so that he did not have to pay for one! Cameras then were 16mm using film stock not videotape.

Gwynne Roberts, a Reuters news agency correspondent met Nick Downey in northern Iraq's Kurdistan in 1974/5. Gwynne takes up the story:

> I met Nick Downey and we subsequently travelled together to Eritrea in 1975, the region of Ethiopia that had been fighting for independence since 1961 [and gained it in 1993]. We walked across it, him with a Bolex [a clockwork, small, Super8 or Standard8 camera that took ¼ inch film, rather than ¾ inch that the professional cameras used; it was light, and simple to use]. I was still a journalist then and although I had on my return a three-part series of articles published in print, the impact of Downey's film was so much bigger, if you wanted to change the world. So it made sense to me: you got paid a reasonable amount of money and then could work on the next project.

Gwynne Roberts

Status

Gwynne joined Reuters immediately after graduating from university. He worked for them until 1973. He then became a freelance journalist working for the *Sunday Times* primarily, before he moved into film. He worked first as a lone VJ then as a single camera operator for Frontline in conflict zones and then as a producer/cameraman making documentaries. He still does this today, now an award-winning documentary maker.

His story

In 1981 for my first trip alone, I bought a Canon Super8 camera and went to Northern Syria. Super8 was film, and each reel lasted just two and a half minutes and I didn't have that many, so I had to be very disciplined. For an interview I only got one 'take', as I couldn't afford to splurge. So you worked out exactly what you wanted, talked to people first about the question and answer and then said, 'tell me what you've said and keep it short'. My objective was to find the British engineer who'd been kidnapped by the Kurds inside Iran, which was at war with Iraq.

My Kurdish contacts helped me float across the river border on the inner tubes of a lorry. We walked and walked for four months, through Turkish lines, me plus two militia men. We passed convoys of lorries going into Iraq supplying them for the war against Iran, through the *cordon sanitaire* or safety zone where you got shot if caught. I got into Iran disguised as a Kurd and about 100 miles in from the frontier I found the engineer. I was smuggled out again and reached Ankara in Turkey to fly home. This trip was all for a *Sunday Times* newspaper commission where they had agreed to pay me £200 per week for six weeks, not four months. My film footage didn't arrive for a month as the Kurds had to smuggle it out through Tehran via the Syrian embassy and then to the UK. Thames TV, one of the major ITV companies in 1982, were interested in using it for their *This Week* current affairs programme, but the broadcast unions wouldn't let it on the screen, because I was not a union member. Then they agreed to allow 1 minute and finally 12 minutes. Peter Gill, one of the staff journalists, had to 'top and tail it' [introduce it and sign off the piece] as well as voice it. So there I had been through heaven and hell, brought back some good footage and found a man suspected of having been killed, only for the unions to say, 'we don't agree with it being shown'.

I love doing this sort of assignment, I can't stop it, and I get turned on by a difficult story. If you get results, it's great, it just seems the natural thing to do. I have done a fair amount in Angola doing frontline reporting, trekking for hundreds of miles with guerrillas and thinking it was the best thing, but I went it alone into some of the conflicts in Africa and it scared me to death. You have to question why you're doing it and nothing compares to an important human rights story. But it should be the story driving you, not the risk, that vicarious pleasure or thrill of it. Because if anything goes wrong you ask, why have I done this? Run the risk of bullets and bombs or being killed?

Illustration 3.1 Gwynne Roberts

On filming technique

I've always used small cameras as they have huge advantages; they're more manageable, more intimate and it feels more authentic. If the shots are grainy and less focussed people don't mind as long as the story is strong. With a big camera on a tripod you immediately get into a set way of filming. You lose something, and although I do use tripods, I think hand-held is good. You can build a relationship with people, you can whip out a small camera when things grab you. I started with Canon Super8, then Sony Ordinary8, moved onto the Hi8 and today I use the new HDTV Sony Z1. Even as a documentary maker, which I became and have been now for over 20 years, I find the small cameras are brilliant. Broadcasters do expect higher picture standards in the UK, but if the story is good and you get access to someone, then it's horses for courses; as ever, it all depends on the story.

I remember interviewing Rafsanjani alone for ITN once using a big camera. It would have been so much better with a crew. [Akbar Hashemi Rafsanjani served as President of Iran from 1989 to 1997, losing on the second ballot to Tehran Mayor Mahmoud Ahmadinejad in the 2005 Iranian presidential election in his attempt at a third term in office.] I was petrified I'd have a technical problem and it is important to be able to relax into the interview and not worry about the camera. For a long while I worked alone, and then I craved working with a crew and then went back to being almost alone. But I now think that to do really good work, two people make a better film than one. As to the pictures, of course there is a difference between a good cameraman and myself. I know what I want and can go and get it, but for a good cameraman each sequence is a work of art.

Gwynne has gone on to specialise in documentaries about the Kurds. He has done four major films about them, winning a number of prestigious international awards. He believes that concentrating on one story has allowed him to report on the Kurds' struggle for independence and record it for posterity. It has also given him a valuable archive of unique footage.

Sue Lloyd-Roberts

Sue Lloyd-Roberts, an ITN staff reporter, went with Gwynne on one of his trips to Armenia. He took a Video8 camera with him and taught her how to use it. She has gone on to become what many describe as the 'Queen of the VJs', winning countless awards.

Status

Sue Lloyd-Roberts joined ITN in 1973 as a news trainee immediately after graduating from Oxford. She remained at ITN until 1981 as a reporter, where she was their first videojournalist, reporting at the start from the USSR. She moved to the BBC in 1992. Her reports first appeared on BBC One's *Breakfast News* where she specialised in human rights and environmental affairs. Her awards:

- 1993 Best Television News category at the British Environment and Media Awards.
- 1995 Royal Television Society Award for International News for her coverage of the plight of China's prisoners for *Breakfast News*.
- 1995 Amnesty International's Television News Award for investigating China's Laogai labour camps, again for *Breakfast News*.
- 1995 European Woman of Achievement by the European Union of Women for her outstanding work investigating abuses of human rights.
- 1996 ITN News and Current Affairs Award at the Sixth Annual Women in Film and Television Awards ceremony for her work on human rights and environmental affairs.
- 1998 Television News Category at the One World Awards for her undercover film from Burma for *Newsnight* proving direct involvement between Western business and Burma's illegal ruling military regime.
- 2000 Television News Category at the Amnesty International Awards, this time for a *Correspondent* film from Nepal which profiled the case of Min-

Min Lama, a 14-year-old girl who was imprisoned for being raped and forced to have an abortion.

- 2001 Actual International Award at Newsworld 2000 Barcelona for her *Correspondent* investigation into the sex trafficking business.
- 2001 Television News Category at the One World Awards for her *Newsnight* report on the displacement of the Masai people in Tanzania.
- 2002 Documentary Category at the One World Awards for a *Correspondent* film on working children in India.
- 2002, Sue was appointed an MBE in recognition of her twenty-five year contribution to international investigative television reporting.

Her story

The advent of Video8 revolutionised TV news because it allowed us to travel as tourists to places totalitarian regimes did not want us to visit. In the former Soviet Union, President Gorbachev literally closed the doors on the republics where there was trouble. Gwynne Roberts and I went to one of these, Armenia, shortly after a demonstration of 1 million people in the streets protesting at the environmental damage done to the region by the Russian production demands. The population of Armenia was then only 2 to 3 million, so it was a huge show and the world did not see it. As there was more trouble expected on Armenian Remembrance Day, we set off posing as Mr and Mrs Roberts (our surnames being conveniently the same). We invented an Armenian godfather wanting us to visit. The

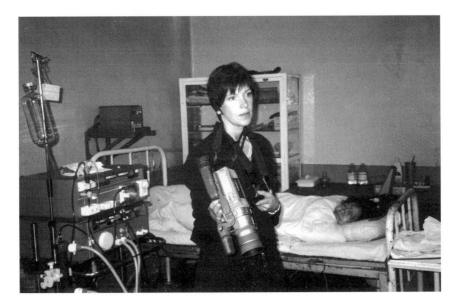

Illustration 3.2 Sue Lloyd-Roberts in China

Illustration 3.3 Sue Lloyd-Roberts in Sri Lanka

diaspora were allowed home because they brought much-needed foreign currency, usually dollars. We met up with an American flight in Paris full of Armenians from LA and flew into the capital Yerevan. Gwynne filmed and I was on a learning curve then. We got good footage, and also were given amateur footage of the demonstration that we transferred onto our camera. We got eyewitness accounts of the Soviet brutality and so brought back a strong story. Gwynne reported a longer piece for Channel 4 News and I did one for *News at Ten*. The camera was basic and the quality of the footage not good, but an exclusive is an exclusive and it didn't matter what it was like. It was seen as the first evidence that the Soviet Union was possibly crumbling. The footage sold round the world. The whole experience changed my professional career, as I didn't much enjoy working with crews and I felt this was my kind of reporting. I never looked back. I have reported and filmed so many stories not only from the former Soviet Union and Eastern Europe but also from Tibet,

Burma and China, Sri Lanka and Nepal. I've specialised in human rights abuses, filming child labour violations, sex trafficking, the sale of human body parts, concentration camps hidden inside China and a good number of environmental stories about the destruction of countries' eco-systems. Why? Well because it mattered to me that so many people were suffering and living under appalling regimes and in difficult environments, where I knew TV could maybe accelerate change or world reaction by showing what it was like. I knew that as a VJ I had the power to help change things or at least to get things moving. One report I am proud of because it did make a difference is that of Min-Min Lama, a 14-year-old girl who was imprisoned in Nepal for being raped and forced to have an abortion. She was sentenced to 19 years. I went on a three-day trek to confront the woman who had induced the abortion and she confessed on camera, so that Min-Min was released. Moreover the Nepalese law was changed so that for rape and under age sex, abortion is permitted. Min-Min is now a dressmaker in Kathmandu.

On filming technique

The cameras got more sophisticated, the Hi8 was followed by the VX1000 and luckily the size of the cassettes got smaller, as when filming on undercover stories I had to smuggle tapes out on my body. My notoriety in TV news is how I put tapes in my knickers to get them through customs and it was true! I did use a tripod as it was lightweight and looked pretty amateurish. I'm not a natural photographer or cameraperson and I learnt everything from ITN editors in the edit suite, the way to tell a news story, the technique of sequences and shots that tell a story. They'd say to me, 'Where is the cutaway, why didn't you do this or that'. Their diktat was always start with a gv (general view or wide shot), then film the details. News means you have to tell a story quickly, so you need a lot of shots, short ones, not zooms but static shots. Being a VJ became a natural thing to do, the marriage of pictures and words, and I felt empowered by holding a camera. When out with a crew, you could ask some cameramen to shoot in a particular way, but the old guard would not – they shot and you watched. There are two key advantages of working as a VJ, firstly you can get into countries and secondly you can get so much more out of interviewees, without having a crew around. There is an intimacy that can develop because the camera is small and unthreatening. Many people cannot imagine that by talking to you their conversation will be beamed to millions worldwide; of course you have to safeguard against that. In Communist and former Communist countries, appearing with a two-man crew was too conspicuous. Interviews and pieces to camera are the most difficult to film alone. For interviews the eye-line is important, so I put the translator in the interviewer's seat, although I remember someone who used a glove puppet as a way to get the eye-line right! You can't guarantee someone won't move so sitting next to the camera is risky – well, I find I can't do it. For pieces to camera, you can do all sorts of tricks like putting a leaf where to stand and then it blows away, or you film and find on replay that children popped up behind you making faces. Often I got a soldier to film for me. My rationale being that if he can aim a Kalashnikov, then he could point a camera. So I'd start off saying, 'hi mum, hi dad' and then speak the real words, hopefully having lulled his suspicions.

Sue Lloyd-Roberts left the BBC in 2006 and now works as a freelance for a range of the BBC's news and current affairs programmes including the Ten O'clock News and Newsnight.

Vivien Morgan

Vivien Morgan (author of this book), a former producer/director of documentaries, went with Sue Lloyd-Roberts to Romania in the winter of 1989.

Status

I worked first in 35mm documentaries, then newspapers as a freelance journalist. I co-wrote *The Alternative Prospectus to Universities* (1975) and this led to me joining the BBC, first as a researcher on Panorama. I went on to train as a TV producer/director at BBC Features. I moved to ITV in 1979 working for a number of companies, as one of the few female directors in commercial TV current affairs and documentaries. I had been at *Channel 4 News* and knew Sue Lloyd-Roberts from before, so it seemed a good combination of our talents to travel together as VJs. We worked together and alone as videojournalists from 1989 until 1994. I continued working as a VJ sporadically and still shoot reports on a small dv camera. I have since lectured in broadcast journalism at university and train VJs as well, mainly in Africa.

My Story

The first time I realised how useful a small camera could be to a story was in 1987 when I borrowed a Sony Video8 and filmed covertly Tahitians arriving at Charles de Gaulle airport on their way to medical treatment in military hospitals. It was the first proof that the nuclear testing in Tahiti by the French had resulted in a huge number of rare cancers and deformed babies in the Tahitian people. I filmed over six months in Paris, meeting patients and the priest receiving them, then followed their stories back to Tahiti. There I used a crew posing as tourists who also shot on small camera. The documentary film won awards but without those cameras we would never have collected our vital testimonies.

My second outing as a videojournalist was with Sue Lloyd-Roberts, a friend and ITN colleague. On our first day filming, we dropped the camera in a department store in central Bucharest and watched it clatter down a steel escalator that was thankfully stopped as there was no electricity in the store. Picking it up, we were in despair: having got into Romania, to return without pictures would be unthinkable. Our assignment for ITN was to get shots of destroyed villages and the testimonies of people, part of President Ceausescu's plans to build a new city and suburbs suitable for his reign. There had been newswire agency reports of what was going on but no pictures had come out. Luckily we found a French-speaking film camera repairman, who mended the camera, but it brought us to the attention of the police.

That meant we were constantly followed and arrested as we tried to get general shots. We did manage one trip to the site of the villages that had been destroyed and to shoot a good deal of wobbly hand-held shots while keeping the car door open to shield us from view. We were also fortunate to get interviews with villagers (using basic Romanian) who confirmed their villages had been destroyed. Arrested around nine times in five days we got our footage out via a 'pigeon' or friend who flew into Romania also on the pretext of a skiing holiday. Far from

Illustration 3.4 Vivien Morgan in Iran

Illustration 3.5 Vivien Morgan in Burma

Illustration 3.6 Vivien Morgan in Eastern Tibet

being put off by the experience, we were so boosted by the amount of world sales to broadcasters we made from our unique footage, despite it being wobbly and rather green-hued grainy images, that it spurred us on to further projects. Romania, post the revolution, sadly offered up a number of stories: the orphanages where children were kept under appalling conditions chained to their beds and in open 'dying rooms' that had no walls so that children were left to freeze to death. Also the Aids babies who were dying as I filmed their plight, the leper colony hidden in the Danube delta, the fight by the Moldovan Popular Front to join with Romania and so it went on. A positive story was returning after the avalanche of Western aid to help the orphans and finding at least one home where children were dressed in proper clothes, surrounded by toys and being let out of their cots to play.

Travels to all the Central Asian 'stans' were the most memorable in terms of reports. The local people, as opposed to the Russians who had been sent there as administrators or encouraged to emigrate, still often dressed in ethnic clothes and were fighting each other – village against village – as they had done for centuries. They were also shaking off the yoke of the Soviet occupation. So the KGB were there to stop me filming, but the Kazakhs, Uzbeks, Kirghiz and Turkmen did not want foreigners around either. No one liked or trusted the sight of a video camera, but in the markets and on the side streets of towns, in the desert at the camel markets and in people's houses it was possible to film. In a number of cases I travelled with a Russian-speaking student, entering burning villages, filming scenes of fighting but also everyday lives in a part of the world unknown to television viewers. We moved across borders, in and out of closed areas disguised as locals, the camera in a plastic bag.

What were the important stories? Well one was going to the Russian town of Ust-Kamenogorsk to report on the (then) most polluted place on earth. It reprocessed the nuclear waste from the nearby nuclear stations and there was no protection anywhere for the people. The nascent green movement had a machine to register the radiation levels. They were way above acceptable levels, the equivalent of what was found around Chernobyl. The film was shown worldwide.

Filming the Romanian children as described; a film of the forced sterilisation of Tibetan women by the Chinese that was shown at the Beijing Women's Conference as evidence by the Tibetan delegation; filming in Burma the use of 'slave' labour in the cities and showing the beautiful country closed by a military junta – the list is, like that of so many other VJs, a long one, so many of the stories forgotten now, but the common theme was recording a changing world, human rights abuse, and telling stories for and about people, to a TV audience that did not know.

On filming technique

Although a qualified TV producer/director and union member, I had never picked up a movie camera before my trip to Paris in 1987. The unions did not allow it. However, I knew the principles of what shots were needed to compile a report: the way to film a sequence, the wide shot, cutaways, close-ups and how to hold a shot for at least ten to fifteen seconds for editing purposes. I also knew that steady shots were requisite and a tripod preferred. In Paris at the airport, filming illegally, it was, however, hand-held shots and crouching down next to arriving Tahitians sick with cancer who were coming for treatment and being whisked to military hospitals. Back to the theory and yes, interviews needed to be shot on a tripod with a relevant background, as did pieces to camera. All this went straight out the window when faced with the pressures of filming as detailed above, or in a 'closed' country where the secret police were always behind you and you were arrested even for filming Ceausescu's newly-built palace, which was regarded as a tourist attraction. So my hand shook, we tried to use the tripod but had to get shots as best we could, from the car window or from far away using a doubler lens that enlarged the camera's standard zoom. As the cameras got better my shooting technique improved. I learnt to hold my breath while doing hand-held to keep the shot steady, to lean against a wall or post to help keep still. The V5000 and then V6000 cameras could be held on your shoulder giving more stability. They were also easier to track with, resting them on a car window-sill and on your lap or hand, carrying it low down to get people's feet, for example. I learnt just how many shots and how much footage was needed to make up a report and that you could never have enough gvs or general views/shots. Sound was a problem at first, because you didn't want to appear obvious by using a hand or stick microphone, so I got into the habit of using a clip or tie mike that had long lead extensions. The only problem with this was that in many Eastern European and Soviet offices the rooms were bugged or wired, so the cable on the floor picked up strange voices and noises! Doing your own piece to camera was, as others have described, very difficult, getting the right head level, making sure the sound was alright. Checking and playing back each take is vital because otherwise you land up like I did once on coming back from Vietnam. The pieces to camera were impossible to use as I had not heard an aviary of birds hidden behind my chosen spot that drowned out my words. In extreme temperatures in Russia and Central Asia the camera fogged and misted up as you stepped in and out of the snow and you had to take time to let it adjust or warm up. In extreme heat or cold the camera just seized up and the batteries ran down at a much faster rate. A few grains of desert sand getting into the camera could stop it working too.

So a back-up camera became essential for travelling in remote places. Sometimes I managed to borrow cameras when my one broke down, as in Belgrade, from a cameraman at the local TV station who was killed a few months later.

You have to take screwdrivers, dust cloths, tape and all sorts of extras to tighten the tripod or tape it if it snapped, which it often did, and to keep the camera going. In extremis a pencil or biro was needed to rewind the tape when it got stuck or a crease in it. Shots were too valuable to give up on! Also a wide angle lens gave different shots, plus the doubler to help with longer distance shots. A good many tanks, soldiers and official buildings like prisons were captured on the 'tight' or full extended zoom lens in this way. A polarised lens or UV filter too to keep the extremes of sunlight from affecting the shots and to protect the lens. Low light, especially at night in rooms lit with a single low watt bulb, did not present too big a problem as the cameras were from the start, even the Hi8, able to record in low light levels, as long as you were on the manual setting and kept the shots close-up. They were grainy, but the story and the content of the interview outweighed the quality argument. Indoors was and is, in some situations, the safest place to do interviews, so you had to either use a still camera light, holding it to the side, or getting someone to hold it to light a face. As the products developed, a camera-mounted light could be used that then cast everything else into shadow. However, this took precious battery power. If you forgot to white balance on the early cameras for fluorescent or interior light, the result was green pictures which were impossible to correct. Batteries were of course vital and they did not respond well to extremes of temperature, dying fast in both cold and heat. If you weren't technically minded and able to plug onto a car battery (for which you in any case needed a car), the local electricity either did not exist or was erratic or too low a charge came through. Cigarette lighters in cars could be used to plug in chargers, but these often failed to produce a good charge. So economy of filming was imperative. Nights were disturbed, on some stories, by having to wake up and change the batteries on charge.

It was all technique learnt on the job, and the bonuses were: in South East Asia or Africa having strong sunlight as the best natural lighting; finding quiet places for interviews and managing to get your material back safely. Everything rested on those tapes, your fees, the next trip and also your reputation. The worst moments were waiting to see them transferred onto Beta for editing and then seeing exactly how bad or good they were. The resulting report had to be worked round the pictures and interviews.

Conclusion

Some of these problems continue for present-day filming. The cameras have improved a great deal but things like circumstances and temperature extremes still prevail. This means that the higher your level of technical expertise the greater the chances of you achieving useable material in terms of pictures and sound. How do you learn this? Partly through trial and error as so many of us did 'in the field', but more by trying to edit it, whether by yourself on a PC software programme or sitting with an editor and seeing where you do not have the shots to cover the journalistic points you are making. So marrying the story to the pictures is the steepest learning curve there is. The next time you go out, you remember your technical checklist but also a mental checklist of shots needed: the variety, length and always more than you imagine you need. I believe a law of filming exists where you can never have enough shots. This because filming the report or story is one thing, but when you get it back to edit, you know that the balance or emphasis of the story has changed. So in some sections or sequences you need more shots to cover commentary or to make the point. No film structure or idea remains the same on paper or in theory once you get out there and start actually recording. So having to be flexible and accommodate change is important, and the ease with which you can work is helped by the small cameras too.

Dan Damon

Status

I'd been going to Hungary on holiday for a few years and thought something interesting was happening there, as there'd been the first multi-candidate not multi-party elections. So I thought, why not stay. I became the sixth person to be accredited as a freelance journalist in Budapest.

His story

Not many months later, in 1989, everything started happening. As it turned out Hungarians were very useful as they used to be the dominant power with their Austro-Hungarian Empire, so you could always find someone living in surrounding countries. For example, in Yugoslavia, a 'fixer' I found was a Hungarian ethnic from Serbia, an old newspaper journo who had good relationships with the Serbs and could drink any one of those hairy guys with guns under the table.

In 1989 I lost about four Hi8 cameras to the East German police who confiscated them from Hungarian freelancers I'd sent in to get stories. The extraordinary thing was that after the collapse of the Berlin Wall I had them returned very properly, without the tapes of course. My two big exclusive reports were from Albania in 1992, when for seven days I was the only reporter with a camera on that story. I got tapes out by sending a guy to the border to hand over tapes. The other was in Sarajevo at the beginning of the war in 1992. On 2 May the bombardment happened and BBC and ITN left, so I was the only one there to cover the story and get the pictures.

Illustration 3.7 Dan Damon

On filming technique

Videojournalism for me was the opportunity to work alone and be as flexible as possible and as light on your feet as possible. I was using Sony Betacam cameras, because I was a freelance VJ and felt I had to film and sell quality pictures. I could manage to lug the heavy camera around, but I was short of money, so I needed to establish myself with the news agencies and didn't want to be seen as a well-meaning freelancer; I wanted to be considered a professional. That way I could get continuing news contracts.

I only used Hi8 when being chased by the police. Hi8 cameras had this vibration as soon as you zoomed in on anything, so could hardly see anything because of the blur. But they were not bad in evening shots. We called it the 'toilet camera' as you could go into a toilet, switch off the light and still get the shots! The unreliability of this new technology could be frustrating with bits of sound equipment breaking, so I quickly learned to carry with me spares for everything. On the serious side of filming, you had to think through the shots. I didn't in the early stages but soon learned that a 40 second shot was better than lots of 3 second ones which you couldn't use for editing. You also learnt to use movement not to avoid it, because you can move much more quickly with small cameras and showing it sometimes made the point of the report. For pieces to camera, I usually got the fixer to stand facing the camera with a tape box on his head, so I could line up the shot, as I was so much taller than everyone else. This didn't always work; for example, once in the Kurdish area of Turkey, I recorded two different pieces for safety, but when I got back and viewed the tape, behind me was a guy picking his nose on both takes, so that one didn't make it.

I loved the idea of working alone, which wasn't always sensible editorially but technically it was fine. You did lose the thinking time by having to do everything yourself. However, editorially you can make mistakes on your own, you can lose touch with reality and that can become dangerous. Yugoslavia, for instance, was known as the motorway war. You could get on the boat at Dover, could be a Tim-Page style journo [he was a photojournalist in the Vietnam War who was killed] taking risks. I knew two or three videojournalists who didn't make it. You see it was too tempting to take the risks to get the pictures and to get them on the news bulletins in the UK. I don't know if you can ever stop people doing that. In Croatia it was easier working alone, not completely alone, not doing a 'Rory Peck', I needed local fixers. [Rory was a cameraman who concentrated on filming difficult wars like Afghanistan, Bosnia, the first Gulf War and the many armed conflicts that followed the break-up of the Soviet Union. He was recognised for his courage and his footage. Following his death in action in 1993, The Rory Peck Trust was established to support videojournalists and freelance camerapeople in the field] I just found it was easier to film, choose shots and edit them as you knew what you were shooting for and it got done more economically and quicker.

Dan Damon is today a presenter of BBC radio programmes.

Vaughan Smith of Frontline

Status

I was in the army and then I tried as a microlight pilot to sell the planes to the Pakistan army, with cameras mounted on them. Anyway they weren't interested. Then I was offering satellite communications and they wanted me to fly dishes in by microlight – absolutely barking.

Then I flew in a photographer Thierry and got some footage of some action, I so enjoyed it and thought this is the life for me.

His story

Rory Peck, a cameraman, was already in Pakistan and when the Afghanistan government attacked Jalalabad in 1989 he got the footage on a Hi8 camera and it was bought because it was exclusive. He and I then went to Romania and he started shooting events again with his Hi8 camera and was selling his footage well, so we formalised the setting-up of a small company that we called Frontline News, in Bucharest, Christmas 1989, over a lot of wine in a hotel. We became the first agency to use these small cameras as a commercial exercise, to get an advantage over the staff news teams. A lot of crusty old cameramen thought we weren't professional at all. However, we managed to sell our footage. We then became more professional as we moved into shooting war or conflict footage, which grew into making actual features of up to 12 minutes long. We had to develop skills to do this and make journalistic judgements about what was a good story, what elements to include and it was by trying to expand our market that we had to think about the journalism. In 1989 we were just opportunists; young men with too much energy. We moved to where the stories were, to Bosnia in 1991–3 and in the first Gulf war I shot the only unofficial footage I know of, using Hi8. It would have been impossible to get that footage with an ordinary camera. All the US soldiers had still photographic cameras, so mine also looked like a consumer item. I used an old army uniform, forged an ID card and took along two Hi8 cameras. I made enough money out of that, about £200,000 from selling the footage, to set up Frontline properly. We were all out there: Rory Peck got exclusive shots of bunkers being bombed; another colleague Peter Juvenal got those amazing shots of missiles literally flying down the street in Baghdad. I had some trouble with officials, like we all did; they took my camera at

Illustration 3.8 Vaughan Smith in Vukovar, Croatia

customs once but then gave it back to me. I was working for the German broadcaster ZDF at the time and I remember they paid my air ticket but only one way! Perhaps they thought I wasn't going to return. Also I was never invited to do pieces to camera, and it was frustrating because you had done the story but sold it to broadcasters who never acknowledged or credited you. They added their own voices. Even worse was that star presenters or reporters assumed the material belonged to their organisation and put it in for awards. I remember coming in to some reporter's hotel room to deliver stuff and it was like entering a scented heaven after where I'd been living. I smelt rank, and they didn't take you seriously until they saw the footage and then tried to rip you off. We could sell for a lot of money and it gave me great pleasure when you had something they *had* to have. The difference between us and staff crews is that we were inexpensive compared to a three person crew and our style of reporting was different too, as we used to live with local people. We had a vision of a slightly more democratic form of news, led by individuals who risked their lives and livelihoods. It was difficult to arrive in a country without support and no training, no fixer, no translator, but three months later we'd leave with something terrific. We needed in conflict to get close to the person, that's what made us what we were. We didn't live in the Holiday Inn in Sarajevo, we stayed with a family. It compelled you to tell their story. We thought a lot about the ethics, more maybe than most journalists, because we got to know people and we felt a pressure to deliver, to tell their story, report their lives as we found it. We had a tiny footprint compared to the large broadcasters, with no logistical support, but we had time, we were less pressured. We tried to predict stories and, for example, in Kosovo I was there for two months before anything happened. Then it started and the Serbs stopped journalists getting in, but I was already there, so it was easy pickings. You had to get an edge by thinking ahead. In news you don't get many experts, just generalists and getting into the story was a product of the technology of those small cameras. Our ability to get under the story meant we often got our reports on *Channel 4 News* and BBC's current affairs programme, *Newsnight*. But we were the bottom of the food chain. People commented on our way of working and said, weren't we irresponsible? No way. Broadcasters were tricky, they paid us only after three months, they were bullies and said we shouldn't be doing this. We made reasonable money, the same as top staff reporters, but we lost eight people, killed while filming, and were risking our lives more. One was lost in Kurdistan at the end of 1991 and the last one in Baghdad in 2003, at which point I closed the company and wasn't prepared to do dangerous journalism. The reason I opened the Frontline Club is that I strongly believe that journalists own journalism not companies. The club is where journalists can meet and where we have a huge range of activities that reflect their work in the world and their concerns.

Illustration 3.9 Vaughan Smith in Kabul, Afghanistan with Peter Jouvenal

On camera technique

Hi8 meant we were like photojournalists but on video. Photojournalism is much freer and our aim was, aged, as we were, 28, for Frontline to be the Magnum of TV news. The cameras stayed the same price but they got better. They were consumer cameras and designed to break or so it seemed. We got no more than 6 months out of a camera. You were never sure footage didn't have some ghastly line or shimmer across it. In the Gulf War I failed to mask up a camera and the sand got in through the switches and buttons and I ended up only being able to film by holding the camera's side at a particular pressure to keep the tape turning, which was hard. Often you had to take the tape out of the cassette, splice it, tape it and still have something to sell. The small dv camera never had any proper lenses, but the quality got better. The Hi8 camera and its successors enabled a different form of journalism: you could do it alone.

Illustration 3.10 Vaughan Smith in Kurdistan

People-orientated reports are best done with these small cameras and I think we were pioneers of this for two or three years. As I'd been a signals officer in the army I knew about batteries, so I had an adapter that could plug into a cigarette lighter or directly onto a car battery. There were always cars around so there was no need to be without power. I also ensured I had enough tape, to protect the camera against dust, and to cover the red recording light, so it could not be seen. I paid a lot of attention to detail.

We lost the competitive edge of using small cameras, because everyone then started using them, but we still maintained our ability to travel. No one travelled as much as we did, but of course you couldn't do it now because of health and safety regulations.

Vaughan Smith runs The Frontline Club in central London and has a website for independent journalists and camera people to post their video reports on the internet. Many of the early VJs like Ron McCullagh are on the Frontline board.

Ron Mccullagh

Status

I left the BBC after the Berlin Wall fell in 1989, where I had been a radio producer on programmes like *Today*. We set up Insight News in 1990, me and Mark Stukey. We used Video8 and Hi8, as Mark had been filming in South Africa before for SABC and had used a Video8. I believe that the news equation is: the quality of the camera is acceptable when circumstances demand it.

His story

In 1990 we made a documentary in Soweto on the children of the township and I brought out a Hi8 and told Mark this was the next big thing. There we were in Soweto, young men, no piles of technical gear with us to be seen as a threat or associated with conventional TV, so we could get to be friends with people. It was easier to close the gap between us and them. You go into a room and close the door and film. It could be in candlelight as in Soweto, as in one scene I'll never forget when they broke off ends of bottles and stuffed them with a mixture of weed and tranquilliser crushed up and then lit up – and there we were in the middle of it, shooting it and stretching Japanese technology to its extreme but getting footage nobody else could get!

A VJ classic example of getting a story cheaply and fast was in Mogadishu in December 1991. The charity, Save the Children, had offered to fly someone in when it had gone completely mad in there. I rang *Newsnight* and said I'm going and the reply as ever was, 'Well I won't commission you but if you come back with anything we'll put it out'. So off I went on that basis. I interviewed both sides, filmed the hospitals that were unable to cope with the wounded and dying, and did an interview with a Save the Children spokesperson saying, 'Somalia had fallen off the edge of the world'. Then I flew out on a Tuesday and was back in London on the Friday.

I rang *Newsnight* and spoke to the editor who said, 'I won't have any fucking freelancer tell me the agenda of my programme'. I said, 'I'm sorry but I've got some amazing footage you have got to see'. It went out on the programme but without my voice on it.

I personally don't like the term VJ, we should be called PJs, as in my view a production journalist is someone who writes, films, produces directs and edits usually longer reports. I think we do the work of Dickens, the way he wrote about social injustices in the nineteenth century in Britain: we do that around the world. I have no doubt whatsoever that we saved tens of thousands of lives, which somewhat makes up for the fact we didn't make tens of thousands of pounds.

On camera technique

Videojournalism is about journalists getting closer. The camera allowed you to risk your life, because it was more dangerous looking through the eyepiece and feeling safe, than if you're with a conventional crew where someone is watching your back. As a videojournalist you never know if everyone has run away and left you filming. In every generation there will always be people who are single-minded enough, courageous and stupid enough to go out and tell these stories. The technology will keep advancing so that it will get easier too.

Ron McCullagh still runs Insight News.

Gareth Jones

Status

I got my first VJ job in 1991 without having done any camerawork at all! I'd been taken on by BBC World Service TV as a videojournalist on the basis of my recent work with Insight News TV. But although under Ron McCullagh I'd learnt a huge amount, I wasn't there long enough to learn how to use the Hi8 camera as I'd been concentrating on reporting, working with a Hi8 cameraman.

His story

Before starting the BBC job I thought I'd better get to grips with the new Sony Hi8 I'd bought before they sent me out to film on a real assignment. I remember taking my wife to a park in Ealing and trying to film her feeding some ducks. It was terrible. The thing I hadn't understood was when and how to start and finish a shot. So the stuff was classic 'tromboning' – continually zooming in and out, pans, tilts, every kind of moving shot and nothing an editor would find useable. I still can't understand why I was so bad, having edited rushes from dozens of cameramen in my previous life as a reporter. Rather worried, I turned to an old mate and in my view one of the best cameramen I'd ever worked with, David Spence. In a packed one day session he took me through all the basics of camerawork skills and drills that I've used ever since. I'll be forever grateful to him for teaching me the bread and butter disciplines and even today I find myself using little tricks that he taught me. It gave people like me great freedom. I've always loved working with a crew and still do. But shooting your own stories allows you to be fleeter of foot and more flexible than a larger team. A lot of the crews I'd worked with up till then were high-maintenance types and often a pain on foreign jobs. Once you were in a country the small cameras also helped you be less high-profile. I could often smuggle myself into far more dodgy/forbidden areas than if I'd been with a team and a barrow-load of Betacam gear. The other thing they allowed us to do was stay with the story for far longer and also get closer to it. Large teams of people are more expensive to keep on location. I became used to spending weeks on assignment, so I could be there for developments in the story or to get to know the subject matter and the characters a lot better than during a flying visit. Not everyone was keen – especially cameramen! I was often looked down upon by cameramen with their big Sony Betacams. Important interviewees looked askance too, as I remember. When I was setting up my Hi8 in Amman to interview King Hussein of Jordan, his aide looked at my little toy camera with a raised eyebrow and said contemptuously, 'You're interviewing His Majesty on *that?*' It was intimidating at times, but I kept on going knowing the tide was with me. One of my worst experiences was getting mobbed in a marketplace in Kinshasa, then Zaire, in 1991 and it taught me a lesson about filming in this kind of situation anywhere in the world, even in the UK. Filming in the middle of large numbers of people can be very dangerous as things can get out of control very quickly. I had tried to take a shot of the market from some distance (there were looted goods being traded there following a big riot), but quickly one or two

Illustration 3.11 Gareth Jones

Illustration 3.12 Gareth Jones

inquisitive bystanders turned into an ugly mob and before I knew it I had my camera and watch stolen. It was a frightening experience, being surrounded by a baying crowd. Hand-held cameras are easier to steal and trade than big betacams and it was only by paying some soldiers to go into the market to get it back for me that I was able to carry on with the assignment.It taught me not to film on my own in situations where public order could break down, even in the UK.

One of my great passions is architecture and the urban environment. I shot a fifteen minute programme on cities for BBC World. It had lots of action, because my small camera allowed me to scramble quickly to cover some guerrilla-style protests in London being led by environmentalist George Monbiot. I was able to follow and spend a lot of time with these protestors, 'reclaiming the land', in a way that I just couldn't with a crew. Very satisfying, being able to deliver so many different elements for a piece and get something on the air that was way off the beaten track journalistically.

Many journalists too were suspicious, believing in a strict division of labour. One editor of a BBC regional news programme was horrified when I told him I was doing camerawork without the benefit of some official BBC training programme and he refused to commission me. Luckily, the managers at BBC World were far more broad-minded and excited by the access this technology gave them to remote parts of the world or tricky stories. They lapped up my material. From BBC World it would also find its way into network packages.

On camera technique

The technical side is obviously one problem when you start. But it's about getting into disciplines. Based on David's lesson, I wrote down notes for reference, troubleshooting notes and checklists of drills e.g. make sure the tripod is level and at the right height *before* you put the camera on it. Simply by practice these things become hard-wired into the brain, leaving you to concentrate on the other aspects like picture composition and the journalism. Interestingly, I've always found sound for TV much more difficult to grasp than the pictorial side. It's only in recent years that I'm now fully confident with audio. I don't think TV journalists pay enough attention to getting great sound: it can often be vital.

There's a bigger issue for the journalist if you define 'technical' as more than just which buttons to press. Not all journalists can make the progression to VJ because good camerawork is more than technology, it is technique. It's a craft and even an art and not all journalists have 'the eye' to enable their material to rise above the level of just being adequate. Sometimes you'd like a heavier camera for more stable shots. I usually use a tripod to get nice fluid moves and I've hauled around a good quality one – currently a Vinten Pro. But I've found that the Sony Z1's stability and also the steady shot facility are pretty good. As a camera when it's got all the sound gear fitted, is getting pretty close to ideal I'd say. Their lay-out is still not professional: there are too many buttons which you can press accidentally which suddenly bring up useless post production features designed for the amateur. Who knows what shots I've missed while trying to get rid of 'fade' and all the rest of them! In the observational documentary I'm making now on the army in Iraq I'm doing most of the stuff hand-held because fixing a tripod is just too slow. Not only do I think I'm getting away with it, I think it looks more immediate and edgy. At first, I was too newsy in my approach, keeping shots short and a bit choppy. Now there's much more flow in the way I shoot. I let things breathe and move the camera off and onto subjects much more. But you need confidence for this. This style is also becoming more popular in news features, which is great.

Gareth Jones is at BBC Wales. He continues to practise as a VJ.

Will Daws

Status

I went straight out of college to City University to do a post-graduate course in journalism. At college I'd been taught what shots you needed, but had no practice. Then I met a cameraman who had started using a Hi8 in war zones. So in 1992 I left City and went to Liberia when there was a lull in the fighting. There I was straight out of college suddenly interviewing the President and I was there when fighting started again and sold the footage to ITN. I was going to be either a journalist or a stand-up comedian. Did I choose the wrong one? I have an adventurous spirit.

His story

I proposed a story to the independent film company RDF who used to sell reports for freelancers, and as it worked out well I kept doing it for two years. I used a Hi8 camera and learnt on the job with flimsy tripod and no radio mike, just a clip mike for interviews. I realised I could go into places and get up close to the action because I had a small camera. I was not technically minded and still today if asked about some buttons, I have no idea. Being a VJ puts you in the radio bracket, like a radio person you're alone and can go off and do everything, like being a print journalist too. But TV is the most powerful medium and the hardest because you have to get the shots; whereas for papers you can write about it and change names for anonymity, with TV it is harder, you have to show pictures.

I found being a VJ was a huge responsibility that I wasn't prepared for. You have people pleading to camera for help and you have to work out for yourself what kind of story it is, for news or documentary. Is it about an event or a character, whose story are you trying to tell? Some stories now are about the reporter's journey, but there are questions about who is offering you access. Rebels will give it to you in war zones so they get their side shown, and some groups are better at it than others. Can you back it up or confirm the facts and are you wary about the access being given? I was out alone in Burundi, and it was so hard with no one there. There were lots of low-level massacres, and I was seeing horrific images, people telling you things, it was hard to keep sane. There you are parachuting into dramas that are not your war and if you're alone you get sucked in easily and lose perspective. I remember filming in an orphan tent where children were dying and one child holding up a baby smiling away and then I realised the baby was dead. You don't relate to what you're filming, you think of getting the wide shot, but not about what you're doing. So do you put it out of your mind and go on to the next place, or have some sort of breakdown or whatever? The camera acts as a shield in difficult situations and even now I still pick up the camera when what is in front of me is too awful to take in.

On camera technique

The more extreme the images you're getting the less you're concerned about the quality and of course now the quality is getting much better. We use Sony Z1s and PD150 or 170 cameras. I've been at the BBC for five years and use small cameras for documentaries. I went into Zimbabwe for the BBC *Correspondent* programme with reporter John Sweeney, posing as tourists and bird watchers using the PD150 and a hidden camera too. You always say secret filming is the last thing people will imagine you are doing, but in Zimbabwe we had to get street shots. I leaned over to the other side of the car with the camera still in a bag to film a prison exterior. A car pulled up and the guy said, 'Looks like you have a camera in that bag', so John just floored it! Then I produced and shot *Holidays in the Axis of Evil*, programmes that we could only do posing as tourists. In North Korea we were on an official tour and couldn't get off it, but what they're showing you can still ask them things about. Ben Anderson, the reporter, was pretending to be making films for mates back home and so asked lots of questions. The series we do *Holidays in the Danger Zone*, is cheap because it is just a producer and reporter using small cameras. We do use video tape editors though, learning how to do that is one multi-skill too far. Some reporters can edit but I personally think you need an editor. There is always a debate about content and style. Before it was about film versus tape and now Beta versus dv, and HD, when it comes in, will magnify this. I think dv cameras are used incorrectly sometimes to save money but used correctly it can look fantastic because of the greater intimacy. People do feel safer and more willing to talk to a small camera but it is a bigger responsibility as you have to let them know where it's going to be shown and now with the internet you cannot guarantee it won't be shown in their country. So it's a lot harder now because an interview shot in profile or silhouette is not as powerful, but we have to be careful.

Daws is at present the editor of the BBC series: Holidays in the Axis of Evil and Holidays in the Danger Zone.

Nancy Durham

Status

Nancy Durham is a Canadian based in London working as a VJ for the Canadian network CBC.

Her story

In 1991, after ten years working exclusively in radio, I became a television news correspondent for the Canadian Broadcasting Corporation, London based. In TV news most of the material I dealt with was second-hand: pictures from agency feeds and from BBC and ITN news reports. It was enough to put anyone off a career in TV. In radio I had always gathered my own material and I missed doing real journalism. The new and better quality lightweight Hi8 camera was suddenly on the scene and it gave me an opportunity to return to original journalism again. In 1994 CBC assigned a Hi8 camera to me, gave me two days camera training and let me loose as a VJ. My first assignment was on the QE2 ship crossing the Atlantic with 1,000 war veterans coming to commemorate the 50th D-Day landing. I shot and shot until I had a shoe box full of tapes and had to turn it into a short feature! It looked so basic, nothing special, no feeling of access because I had gone out and acted like a cameraman and used a tripod all the time. When I discussed this with my bureau chief, he said throw your tripod out the window, go hand-held, go somewhere between breaking and following the rules, and bring back something special.

In 1995 near the end of the Bosnian war Serbs were expelled from Croatia by the tens of thousands. They fled with whatever they could carry in a wheelbarrow, a car, or a bicycle basket. They were taunted and jeered as they crossed Bosnia on their way to Serbia. I met one convoy as it entered Serbia. I could see no beginning or end to the line of people on the move. The refugees were Serbs but they had no particular affinity for Serbia; some didn't even know anyone there. Emotions were high and there was a sense that reporters were not welcome. I asked my Serbian fixer, Sandra Stajner, if she would ask a group of women – riding in the back of a covered hay wagon being pulled along by tractor – if I could get inside and ride with them. I showed them my small Hi8 camera. They waved me in and Sandra drove the rental car. There was no room for a crew and I didn't need an interpreter in the back of that wagon. The women had a map of the Balkans and were pointing to Kosovo where the authorities had told them to go. I could see their despair. They knew where the next war would be. One of the women held up a set of keys; clearly they were for the home she'd just left and would likely never see again. Filming in the back of the hay wagon that day I knew I had special access. It was close, intimate and very natural. When my pictures went to air the newsdesk back in Canada saw that this was special and they asked for more. I continued to cover the break-up of the Balkans with a small camera (though by the end it was digital and the pictures were much improved) but it was the small camera – and the one-person band – which took me inside the big picture, allowing me to shoot not just up

Illustration 3.13 Nancy Durham in Kosovo, 1998 © Visar Kryeziu

close but also to shoot from the perspective of those fleeing for their lives across the Balkans.

So that's what I do now, try and get across the intimacy that this sort of filming allows you, to get right inside. I've developed a way of telling the story as I'm doing it, with asides to camera during the report, like 'someone told me this … so that's why we're going there'. I so enjoy being a VJ and the freedom it gives me. I can shoot all day and night if I want to and there's no crew saying 'it won't work' if I suggest a shot and I can be more experimental by myself. Being a VJ is a great leveller, people like to help you and, for example, you spend a lot more time with the people you're interviewing and go for meals and build relationships. That's when you get to know each other and talk about your lives.

Dangers? I've always felt fine on my own, but then I've always had to have an interpreter, so I wasn't really alone. I consistently feel safer not being with a big crew, you can jump on a bus or the back of a hay wagon, you can be flexible and move fast. More than that, I am able to do reports from all over because of the economy of working as a VJ. There is no way I could travel the way I do except alone.

On camera technique

Coming from a radio background I understood the need for good sound. It is as important as the picture. I always use both channels on my camera – today I shoot with a Sony Z1 – to ensure my questions are

Illustration 3.14 Nancy Durham in Kosovo, 1998 © Visar Kryeziu

recorded as clearly as the answers I get. It's really important to mike questions properly. Including a question here and there can substitute for a couple of script lines, keeping your writing tighter and giving a natural flow to a report. Also, as a VJ, questions are a strong part of your 'personal presence' in a story. Viewers may not see as much of you on camera as a traditional reporter but *hearing* some of your interplay with interviewees adds to your authenticity – it shows you are really there.

Another tip: it's obvious but a strategically placed wireless mike will pick up two or even three people. If I lock off my camera to roll for a shot with two guests plus myself, I then step into the frame joining the guest(s). In this way I can show my personal presence in a set up shot and I use the wireless microphone a guest is wearing to pick up my questions. It's an easy way to get a decent sound up along with an introductory shot. Whenever I shoot a set-up I always keep the conversation on the interview topic. The camera is usually at a distance at this point and in that environment an interviewee may feel more relaxed and speak less self-consciously, adding that little bit more to the main interview. I find the Z1 more stable and better for hand-held, but I'm thinking about getting a monopod maybe, because you can turn it on yourself if you want to film a piece to camera. I always conduct the main interview on a tripod or using a very steady shot and then ask the subject many of the same questions when I'm moving around hand-held, with him or her as they show/tell whatever it is I'm filming about. This provides nice choices in the edit suite.

Also I find the tripod so heavy to lug around but you have to. It took me years to turn off being the journalist and becoming a camera operator, of not interrupting a good shot with a question. Now I'm still a journalist first and foremost but I also feel like a cameraperson.

Conclusion

The VJ pioneers I've included here are just a *few* of the early ones and this is not a definitive list. There are many others who were there in the field at the same period in1989 who go unmentioned. There were at Channel One, at TVam during the dispute and over the past twenty years many solo camera operators, mainly using professional cameras, who have gone on to become award-winning camerapeople/producers/reporters and no doubt some who have moved to using smaller cameras too. The range of people and their stories described in this chapter are meant to inspire and interest you in just what can be done with small hand-held cameras, by telling you about people who started off using those little black Hi8 cameras and turned a tricky way of working into a new and workable medium of newsgathering. For as each person has said, the camera allows you to be so much more intimate with those you are filming. Time and again in the interviews for this book the word 'intimate' keeps being used. There is no large crew or camera to distance you from the subject or event you are filming. Many of the stories are about filming abroad because it was a time in history where technology and events came together, a unique combination. However, with the growth of local and community TV a different market for videojournalism is growing. This is discussed in the next chapter.

Questions for students

1 What inspired the early VJs to go off and film reports – often in dangerous conflict zones?
2 Did they find the small cameras appropriate for the filming they did?
3 What limitations are there when using small cameras in terms of technique and getting the footage?
4 What are the advantages of having a small camera when travelling, and being a one-person-band?
5 Can you list five rules for shooting that you found useful to read about?

4 Local TV: videojournalists in action

Local TV is being called the last great television adventure because transmitting via the internet as well it can reach communities where people no longer want to watch conventional programming. It is exciting too in that it is also programming by the people for the people using the interactive technology that is now available. All this has been made possible in the UK by OfCom, the governing body of UK communications industry, granting two -year Restricted Service Licences across the country for towns and cities to experiment with local TV programming. This move by the UK government, following in the US's footsteps, is welcomed because it

> Encourages broadcasting by community groups, voluntary associations, colleges and universities as well as by radio broadcasters, smaller television producers, video workshops and access centres. By connecting citizens to one another, it could regenerate a sense of community and combined identity. If combined with the new information communications technologies, it could enable a more responsive, interactive political system to develop at a local level.
> (Dave Rushton, Director of the UK Institute of Local Television)

Why now? Well, the technology is here for this form of broadcasting to be delivered via cable (as in the US) or via TV or broadband. It can be funded by local advertising attracting 'a local audience below the ITV audience', as described by Lindsay Charlton, MD of ITV Meridian and Director of the ITV local project. In fact ITV anticipates it as a stand-alone business that can tap into an estimated £2 billion of local classified advertising across the UK that has, until now, gone to local newspapers. This is a way, Charlton says, of 'getting the internet as TV companies', meaning harnessing the potential and linking it to TV. ITV is working with Narrowstep, a technology company that believes it can deliver quality video over broadband channels and also protect the content from piracy. At the moment, each of the ITV local broadband stations in Brighton and Hastings has seven channels including local news, weather, classifieds and events in the area, with sports being added too. It also has a way for people to send in their own videos – either for advertising or other interactive purposes like entertainment and competitions. The emphasis is on the fact that local events can attract viewers and also people prepared to pay to see complete coverage of events like Cowes Week, the annual sailing competition situated on The Isle of Wight. Again in business terms it is considerably cheaper to launch a local TV channel than one on satellite: around £50,000 versus around £1 million. Apart from the business prospects, feedback from pilots and from channels like Channel M in Manchester – that has been running since 2000 – shows that people like it.

Community TV or cable has been around in the US for some years, but the UK has only now seen its potential. Most importantly though it has found its time and place, coming as it does when the networked generation is no longer watching traditional TV. The latest figures show viewers moving away to online services, downloading content onto iPods and mobile phones, and participating in online communities. The pilots and channels broadcasting vary considerably. The Blackpool Borough Council in the north-west of England had Sony install a digital television studio, costing £250,000, so that it could link to every school, library and council office in the district via a Cisco broadband connection. The local authority is the first public body in the UK to develop the means to broadcast Internet Protocol Television (IPTV), or programmes via the internet. The aim is to broadcast everything from 'TV CVs' and media training for councillors to video recordings of school teachers showing good teaching practice. The studio is large enough to record interviews, news briefings, a small group discussion, or a small drama. A conference room next to the studio has been wired up to broadcast public meetings. The cameras also convert to portable camcorders for location work. Television studio manager Steve Lloyd says 'the studio gives community groups the opportunity to make programmes and get their voice heard on a bigger platform. Blackpool is leading the way towards a new age of community television'.

In Manchester, the Guardian Media Group is running Channel M via TV free-to-air channels and also on the NTL digital cable network. It is linked to CHUM International TV of Canada and the International Media Centre of Salford University. It offers news and American programmes covering music, fashion and behind-the-scenes of film and programme making, broadcasting for six hours per day. It also includes programmes produced by local media students. It runs advertising too.

The largest local TV experiment to date has been carried out by the BBC in the Midlands. This was part of its commitment by Nations and Regions to local programming and involved using thirty-two videojournalists specifically trained for the nine month pilot in 2006. It provided, says the editor David Holdsworth, 'a greater breadth of local news and had an average of 15 more cameras on the ground. We also achieved our target that a quarter of all content would be made by viewers'.

It was deemed successful at combining community involvement with a new style of newsgathering using only VJs. The future of local TV for BBC regions will not be decided until late 2007 when if it gets the green light some 60 local stations could be established. Some of the local newspaper groups in that region and nationwide have reacted strongly to the idea, fearful that they will lose their readers to local TV. It is according to the Newspaper Society a real threat, but regional newspapers like the *Hull Daily Mail* have decided to follow the national dailies like *The Daily Telegraph* and produce video news for their own websites, so challenging the local internet and linear TV channels. The war between print and TV has moved into a new phase, with videojournalism seen as the key.

Before this boom and the local TV pilots, the practice of videojournalism on a commercial or large scale in the UK had been limited to one channel in the 1990s. This was when Channel One, as mentioned in Chapter 1, a cable news operation, was set up. The idea was to use only solo operators who used professional cameras and rode motorbikes to get around London shooting reports. News offices were later set up in regional cities too. As one former VJ remembers,

> Channel One did help people get a foot in the door – such a good training if you can do it all yourself day after day. You know how to put packages together and sell a story, but it is exhausting. I now remind reporters sometimes that you're producing the whole film plus sound and all the nightmares. When recording and trying to do an interview you're also listening to sounds, to the clicks, thinking of the shots – but it is fantastic.
>
> (Will Daws)

For another pioneer VJ, Dan Damon, in London looking for employment at this time, the station seemed a timely opportunity for him to continue practising his craft:

> I came back from Eastern Europe in a hurry and Channel One was not too bad. Nick Pollard, ex-ITN, was editor. Anyway I've always liked motorbikes and I got to drive around London with a camera strapped on my back. It wasn't very grown-up but I enjoyed it. Everything was pre-recorded half an hour in advance of broadcasting. It was shot on Beta. Channel One was fine until the good people went when they saw it wasn't going to work, because they couldn't get on more cable stations. In my opinion, it was over-budgeted and engineered, whereas now with the BBC's local TV, it's more adaptable, helped by the technology, like smaller cameras and pc editing.

To train production staff in preparation for the local TV pilots, the BBC carried out a scheme begun in January 2004 to develop what it called a 'self-op' strategy for the whole organisation, but particularly for the nations and regions. This was to pioneer personal digital production, or PDP, skills for some 300 journalists, teaching them to be able to shoot and edit their own stories using small dv cameras. Like the ITV experiments, local TV has to be financially viable which is why VJs have been identified as the way forward. As Vin Ray puts it,

> It all depends where you're sitting: in network news videojournalism is an added tool, if in Nations and Regions then it is fundamental. It also depends on what you want to achieve and with how much money. Local TV is a different kind of journalism, not just the poorer cousin of network news, but something closer to the community.

The BBC, like ITV, feels it has identified a way to provide communities, who are not served by the large conurbations, with their own TV programmes. More than that, it allows for interaction at a unique level. Using existing radio stations to keep the expenses down, the BBC TV output on the nine month pilot schemes proved achievable and the local material also fed up the food chain into the regional programmes. The rest of this chapter is a description of how local TV operates and how the VJs go about their daily work. It provides a useful guide for anyone thinking about being a VJ, by detailing the VJ's work in particular and how they got started on their career paths. There are also filming tips.

A day in the life of a local TV office

Staffordshire TV is based in the offices of Radio Stoke in the Potteries town of Stoke-on-Trent, in the Midlands. The new office building, facing the Victorian town hall, is well positioned for people to drop by. This is important as there is an open centre downstairs where children can come and make animation films that are then broadcast, and people can come and use the internet and other facilities. This is also where the community producers meet with people who want to make their own reports. Access is a key part of any community-based station.

Staffordshire is a large geographical area to cover, considering the VJ's constraints of having to go out and film and then edit a report every day by 5 pm. The radio newsroom is separate from the VJs or local TV room. A producer sits in the centre of the VJs, overseeing the daily output and working on story ideas and also helping with the post-production, namely scripting and editing. In the garage are the staff cars for VJs to use. Each VJ has their own Sony Z1 camera and kit, with the smaller Sony PD150s available too, that the community and faith producers tend to use most. There are closed booths for recording commentary.

An interview with Sue Owen, MD of Radio Stoke

She explains how the local TV project was set up and run and how it worked with the local community.

> For the pilot we advertised and had 400 applicants for 30 posts (across the whole Midlands region). The idea was to have people from across the board. We already had some people who already had PDP training. Here at Staffordshire TV we have a team of five VJs who all came from different areas of work. One VJ was a video librarian, another was a picture editor and two were ex-radio journalists. The average age of our VJs is 30, so this is not for recent media graduates. The reason being that it is very tough to make a film a day; it would be too steep a learning curve for someone straight out of college. We also have a community producer, whose job is to get stories from the public in three ways: material from media students; by training people on how to use a camera and then help them shoot and edit a story; and finally by getting community groups to come up with ideas for a film, which they then direct but we film and edit. We have four of these UGC [user generated content] pieces transmitted every week. The faith producer makes two to three films per week about faith in its widest sense, and the job is as much about making links with different local groups.

Links with local newspapers

> It depends on who owns which newspaper group in each area across the Midlands. Our local newspaper is *The Sentinel*, owned by The Mail group. There has been no relationship between them and the BBC for over 20 years, but we do work with *The Express* and *Star*. I think the newspapers see us as making tracks on their lawn.

Transmission

> Our output is one ten-minute bulletin per day, that can be viewed on demand on broadband but on DSat it is shown at ten to the hour every hour. It is not rolling news, but if there is a big story, like one we had on a quadruple murder, then we can update it every two hours.
>
> Regional TV uses one or two films from the local TV output in every bulletin. There is also a regional reporter based in the office whose report can go out on local TV if they are doing a relevant story. What it means for the regional news programme *Midlands Today*, is that it benefits greatly, getting an extra 25 to 30 films per day to choose from across the region.

Viewing figures

We have found that what's worked best has been what we call the functions: weather, traffic, news in brief, because they have been very localised and detailed. Broadband figures have been better than TV for example in the month of May. (That is on demand, rather than waiting for the TV broadcast at ten to every hour, so it began to show what people prefer.)

Interviews with the VJs

Stuart Ratcliffe, VJ and output producer, aged 31

CAREER

I did a degree at York in English and Media, graduating when I was 22. It is an industry-connected course and everyone spends time in industry. I spent four months at BBC Leeds, but my first proper paid job was as a station assistant at BBC Norwich in 1992. I put graphics together for bulletins and gallery directed too, which meant pressing the buttons as the bulletins were broadcast live. I kept coming up with strand ideas to show that I could put films together, then I got a couple of newsroom attachments and programme attachments as well as a news camera course, followed by full PDP training.

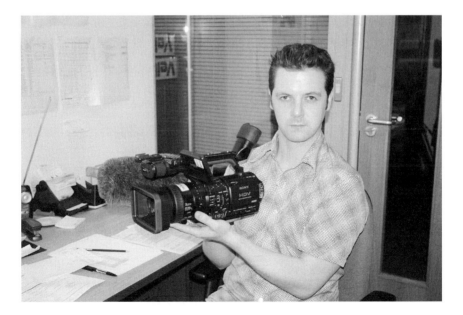

Illustration 4.1 Stuart Ratcliffe

ON FILMING

I volunteered to film my own features from the beginning. I wasn't in
the union though so I was seen as a troublemaker, not by management,
but by the technical people who said you're taking away our jobs (this
was in 1998/9) but I got to do camerawork that way. My first VJ task
was to do an interview at the local theatre. I used a PD150 camera,
with the camera mike. The night before I was so worried that every
frame would be scrutinised, so I made a checklist: remember to white
balance and so on, as I didn't want to slip up. I then had to edit it with
an editor so all my camerawork was seen. It's hard doing it alone. You
get the camera set up and then run round it to do the interview and I
had to get people to give me their name and title, because I'd thought
so much about the technicalities, I'd literally forgotten who the person
was. If you have a cameraman you can warm your guest up and talk
to them, but not when you are alone so I have found a way of asking
a couple of general questions first that I generally don't use, but it gets
people comfortable.

OUTPUT

I always saw myself as a journalist, thinking in terms of stories, but
you always get something more from being a VJ, more of a rapport.
For example, on a factory floor when people talk to you like a mate
even though you're filming them, because there is no cameraman as a
gooseberry. That way you get a better interview and I think our stuff
holds up well to regional stuff done with crews. In style we don't look
formulaic, we look fresher, and, for example, we focus on the person
doing things not just on showing the standard shots. It is different at
a local level, it's got to be about connecting with the audience, people
have to be seen in pieces and they'll then watch, and so will their
friends.

DAILY SCHEDULE

I look at stories from the VJs and have my own ideas that I then use to
write up what is called prospects (i.e. possible ideas we could cover the
next day). I send it in the night before to the radio news editor, who
holds a morning news conference for the radio side and what they will
cover and then we talk to confirm our ideas.

The VJs are fairly sure of their plans by the night before, following
our exchange of ideas and what could be covered, but there can be
changes following the morning's news conference. We have a five-
member team, most of whom go out to film each morning and I help
them with scripting later in the day. We record voice [commentary]

and links into our cameras in quiet booths. Then it is all downloaded onto our pcs and we edit the pieces ourselves. My job is to ensure that BBC editorial guidelines are adhered to and to check for legal issues. Also to remind the team that we don't do what I call advertisements or 'puff' pieces, so even if we are invited to go behind the scenes at an amusement park, for example, we have to be objective and impartial in our reporting. While the VJs are out, I also write, film and edit a news in brief, NIB, every day that goes on air – on broadband and TV that is. Editing is on our pcs using Avid. We name or caption (or Aston, a term used that it is the actual name of the company that makes a caption-generator machine that is installed in most studio galleries) people in our pieces ourselves using a font size Pt42 so they can be read on broadband. We don't really have time to log shots before editing. You have to listen to the interviews as you're downloading and make mental or rough notes. We have dv players on the desks where we can put in our tapes for downloading but our UGC [user generated content] producer often works from home and so she uses her camera to download straight into the laptop. We then send reports to Birmingham down the line feed and router, where it is uploaded onto the website for broadband viewing. Hereford and Worcester are already uploading their material themselves onto the web, but that does mean that editorially stories lose a final check. This could be important at weekends for instance when there is not a full editorial staff and VJs would be uploading straight onto the web without anyone checking their scripts and pictures. The pieces are a maximum of two minutes, usually one and a half minutes, as on the web people are not prepared to look any longer, their attention span is shorter partly because the screen is much smaller to watch. Stories are generally re-cut for online but some interviews rated as worthwhile are run to length. A good tip when shooting for online, choose bigger close-ups that will show up well on the small screen.

AN EXAMPLE OF A VJ REPORT

There was a story in Cambridge of a murder in the village and people thought it was someone from the illegal travellers' encampment nearby. The BBC tried to get interviews with the travellers to get their views, but they never agreed. Anyway the camp was on my way home, and after a month of stopping and chatting to them, telling them that it would just be me plus my little PD150 camera that I showed them, they eventually let me on the site. I spent three days there and got their stories. This wouldn't have been possible with a proper crew, not just in terms of the cost of all that time, but also they would've been intimidated by huge craft cameras. I won their trust and also got an exclusive.

In retrospect I should have done a postgraduate in broadcast journalism, so that I started or came in to TV as a journalist. Those with postgraduate degrees went straight on to news shifts, while I had to go into a more technical grade and work my way across. Media courses give students too high expectations because they do everything on their courses and think once in a job they'll do all those things straightaway. I say to students, 'you can go out and shadow a VJ', and they reply, 'Won't I be doing the filming? I do it at college'. I think it's essential that you have practical skills from any course you take because to be a VJ or a producer or reporter you need to be able to do three things: report, film and edit. It means as a journalist you can film your story, your idea, and it is all your creation. Another tip is to keep a camera in the back of your car, so you can film a fire or something. You never know what might happen. In the future we'll no doubt also have to know how to upload material onto the website because we need to get it up quickly, but it still has to be checked editorially.

Laura McMullan, VJ, aged 30

CAREER

I did a media studies course at De Montfort Leicester University. It was a totally practical course with no journalism elements. The worst part was that I did no work experience so when I came out, I applied for about 110 jobs but had no experience. Then Radio Stoke, whom I'd been in contact with, offered me some phone answering shifts, so I got my foot in the door. Six months after that I became a newsroom PA [production assistant]. Then the researcher/picture editor was leaving, so I said I could edit and I got the job and spent six years editing. During that time I applied for a PDP course. I wanted to be able to do my own stories, to be responsible for the whole process. When local TV came about it seemed such an amazing opportunity, so I applied. I wasn't the most experienced person or a journalist, but I was local which might have helped me get it.

BEING A VJ

Nobody can describe how it takes over your whole life, there are not enough hours in the day. I don't have time even to talk to colleagues, e-mail people, time to research a story properly, it was 'bang bang bang' getting it out for that evening. Every day a report of 1 minute 40 seconds, with pressure when you start in the morning to get it ready to send down the line by 5 pm. Being a one-man-band is hard, so it's nice if occasionally someone carries my tripod for me. There is hardly time even to go to the toilet or get anything to eat, but it is so rewarding as well. Editing is the hardest part and the most time consuming. I try to be creative in my edits not just 'cut cut cut'; it helps by planning to film in a stylish way, thinking ahead and working on tomorrow's idea, not just chasing your tail. I had editing skills but hadn't done any journalism training, so I had to learn that while being a researcher/editor, working for the regional reporter. I'd like to go on a course and be told: these are five basic pointers, things that I should or shouldn't do. I'd never covered a court case, for example, and so when I did a piece on a pending case, I wondered about using a picture of the accused guy. The person I asked in the newsroom went crazy and said 'don't use a picture, you can't'. If something is *sub judice*, I now know you cannot show someone's face. So I'm always checking but I'm happier doing local and what I call 'emotional' stories. To me, local TV is about real people, someone who has done something great for the community. Maybe it won't make it on *Midlands Today* regionally, but that doesn't mean it's not a good local story. I think I am more of a storyteller making a good bond with people, but I'm not sure if I'm a great journalist. Would I ever report from Iraq? No way, you'd never get me in a war zone.

Illustration 4.2 Laura McMullan

At the end of the day maybe you have an hour to put in calls for the next day's story, so there is not much preparation time. Also I like to know what my story is before I go out, so I write out a rough script, leaving room for changes and manoeuvre, but it helps focus me. For interviews it helps me remember what I'm hoping they'll say. I'll set the first location up for 9 am, film for no more than one-and-a-half to two hours tops, get back by 11 am or 1 pm at the latest and then edit.

What do I do when things go wrong and I lose a story? Well you've still got to get a story together. When this happened once, I found a story in the newspaper about the local ambulance service being threatened with cuts. So I phoned and arranged an interview with the Head of the PCT [primary care trust] and then went out on the street filming and asked people what they wanted to know or say about cutting back the ambulance service. I inter-cut their questions with his answers, and used library shots of ambulances and hospitals to underlay my commentary. So I managed it and it worked fine.

ADVICE TO STUDENTS

You have got to be a 'get up and goer' and stay constantly on this level of motivation. It's like nothing you've really experienced before, not just sitting at your desk and wondering what's on for today. It's five stories to deliver, five days a week. Your camera is your extra limb, you never go anywhere without it. The VJ job is everything I ever wanted to do. You have got to love what you do, it is such hard work, but the reward is there. It is not a job for students coming out of university, because you need to be technically very good.

Tim Parker, VJ and faith producer, aged 33

I travelled with Tim on a story that was a forty-five minute car journey from the Radio Stoke office. He was not doing this for the same day broadcast, but was following up a past story about a woman member of the Ionian community who had a garden of different 'rooms' which each represented a stage in Christianity.

CAREER

I did a degree in geography because I didn't know what to do. Then I knocked on the door of BBC Radio Leicester and begged to have a look around, to get some work experience. I stayed there almost five years, started off making tea and ended up presenting programmes. I had to prove at every stage that I could do jobs, by going off and doing extra

Illustration 4.3 Tim Parker

work, recording vox pops [vox populi which are short comments from people in the street usually]. I knew I needed to qualify as a journalist, so I went and taught for five years in Japan to earn some money and then came back and did a bi-media postgraduate course at Trinity All Saints in Leeds. It was heavily slanted towards TV and I got experience using the software I now use, which has been a great help to me. I went back to Radio Leicester and got a contract as a radio journalist and then this job came up and I got it.

WORK AS A VJ

Although I was ready for the challenge, I couldn't anticipate how different working would become. There was the pressure of 'now now now', to turn a story round fast, but I also had to develop relationships, find interesting stories and encourage people to shoot and report stories themselves. Most VJ roles are to turn round stories quickly, but for me it was 'foot off the pedal' more. I did a PDP course when I got this job. I find as a VJ you're dictating the story, you have to know what you need for the package otherwise you won't get the shots. So you have to direct people, needing them to do this and say this in a different way, like paraphrasing your questions in their answers. Sometimes you have to throw the rule book out the window. A tip: when the unexpected happens keep the camera running. When it happened to me the first time I was so surprised that I stopped the camera, so I lost the story. You

Illustration 4.4 Tim Parker

have to find the balance between being a good journalist and getting it right technically. You need to think about lighting, picture composition, artistry, that is the biggest challenge. There is an endless treadmill feeling that comes from having so much to do. It all starts with the story idea but you are the only person to do it, there is no one else. Is it too much? When I first started, quite frankly, yes.

A VJ REPORT

The first story, I made a complete hash of it. It was about a synagogue closing and I had no idea of how I was going to tell the story. But then I stopped panicking, put sequences together in my head, started filming them, thought through the interview, what I needed as soundbites and how to film the interviews. Somehow I got through.

ANOTHER VJ REPORT

Tim returned to the 'faith garden' as the owner had suggested coming back in the summer and the original piece had been well received. The gardens are unusual. The 'resurrection' garden features a ten foot black wooden cross in a black-pebbled bed, surrounded by red plants and is extremely dramatic. This time, he walked round looking at possibilities with the woman priest. They finally agreed on the 'passion' garden and Tim got his PD150 camera and tripod out. He did not mike-up the speaker, but relied on the camera mike. She spoke to camera describing the different plants and then he got her to walk in the garden, showing those plants mentioned, and he filmed the plants separately. This allowed him the choice of using her voice over the pictures and adding commentary if need be. He looked for an opening shot and an end shot to finish the piece. He took his time to make sure he filmed plenty of extra shots to use. There was, as he said,

> a reason for every plant and flower, so it is a kind of *Gardeners' World* piece but people love it. Also it is what I call a reflective story, so you expect an image-packed, fast-cut piece, but it is slower and viewers like this sort of piece.

The filming took around an hour and a half and then there was the same drive back to base. So it took a total of around three hours and unless he had started early in the morning he would not have got the piece ready for that evening, if it had to be an 'on the day' or 'same day' piece. It proved the pressures of being a VJ, of working against the clock, and fitting everything in.

TIM'S ADVICE TO STUDENTS

> Do not overlook the technical side; you think there'll be someone to look after that side. There used to be, but now there isn't, it's all down to you. So you have to get training of some kind before you apply to be a VJ or even a TV journalist, in my view.

Conclusion

Has local TV got a future? That is the question being asked by those who have taken part in the BBC pilot. 'If I had my way I would want it to go on; we have had such fantastic feedback', says Sue Owen. The future of these community-serving channels lies with the accountants and if they say it is viable and can be achieved either through advertising on the commercial stations or within the BBC's budget, then it appears that they have a future. The viewers, according to the pilot projects, are there both online and on TV.

Videojournalism at this level has brought plenty of positives, but also a number of negatives too. The broadcasters can cut costs to the bone and believe that multi-skilling like multi-platform is the way forward. The question is, can this be achieved without any other costs in terms of quality and journalism standards, let alone labour relations? The VJ role has thrown up potential problems. 'Some people are good at the filmmaking side but not the journalism, while other journalists have no visual skills. If this is rolled out, we need to address this', says Sue Owen. Vin Ray from the BBC College of Journalism would agree with this because as he says,

One theme has emerged from the experiences of videojournalism and that is that you still have to be a good journalist whether doing it yourself or with a camera operator. What you get when non-journalists do it is not good enough'.

As my visit to Staffordshire TV showed, the VJs were all enthusiastic and took the challenge of being on a five day treadmill with fortitude. However, it is an exhausting and perhaps unsustainable level of output; some fat needs to be left on a newsgathering operation. It appears too lean, especially when faced with the growing competition in the form of local councils developing their own media projects like Blackpool, independent internet channels beginning to emerge offering services and programming at local level and newspapers developing multi-media websites. The good news is that journalists who have video-making skills are in demand on an unprecedented scale.

5 The way news is produced

In this chapter we look at how news is produced and how the demands of unbundling news means that the updating of stories is now almost continuous for multi-platform delivery: online or via 24 hour news channels. Still the basic workings of a newsroom and the 'grammar' of newsgathering remain and the role of an editor, whether for a TV programme or online news bulletin, is arguably even more critical at a time when the amount of information is growing. Sifting through and selecting stories has traditionally been part of the news production process, so is the way that material is collected and then produced to tell and show the viewer what is happening. This is the prime role of newsgathering and it applies to newspapers having to compile their daily publications, to weekly magazines and to any agency in the business of delivering news.

Let us look at a news operation whose hub is the newsroom. Whatever the kind of channel or organisation, or size of output, the structure is the same. A news desk headed by the news editor and supported by a team consisting of producers, reporters, crews and technical staff, especially VT (video tape) editors. Into this mix can also be added a VJ, who can be called a 'self-op', 'shoot/produce' or multi-skilled production person.

The structure

The news editor is in charge. It is up to him/her to decide on which stories to pursue, to headline, to maintain or discard.

The editor is restricted in choices by a number of factors – most of all by time.

You might wonder how deadlines and timing can remain the same if a channel is running 24 hours a day. The answer is that what has changed is the number of teams working in shifts to supply two- or three-hour sections for that 24-hour operation. So it requires more teams of the same mix of people. Also time is still the driving force because no output is unstructured and while the programme may lose items to accommodate a breaking or rolling news story that gathers pace during the day, on a quiet day without a big story there are still hours of airtime to fill. Of course news bulletins and headlines on the hour exist outside the 24-hour format and are broadcast at set times, as programmes of 2, 5, 10 or 30 minutes. The stories the news editor chooses to include, apart from the main ones that are dictated by events, may be affected by his or her preferences, e.g. for human interest stories rather than foreign or crime. But there is a wider agenda that helps define which stories are or are not included; for instance, channel ownership, where the bulletin is broadcast, the time of the bulletin, and the type of bulletin or programme e.g. rolling news, lunchtime news or the main evening news. We will look at these factors later in more depth.

First though, how do the day's stories and events come together into a news bulletin or programme?

The newsgathering process

It breaks down into four different areas:

- Planning
- Gathering
- Selection
- Presentation.

The news editor has a goal: to fill the bulletin – but this is in itself a constraint, as each bulletin has a set length, as mentioned earlier. So not all the stories can fit in and they have to be ranked and given a time-value. If you look at a running order in the Appendix you will see how carefully each item is timed. A story's duration indicates its newsworthiness.

When is this decided? At the morning meeting or first meeting, according to the bulletin's expected broadcast time. So it is the night before for a breakfast bulletin which is worked on by the overnight team who will hand it over to the morning team at perhaps 6 am. At 10 am work starts on an early evening bulletin; midday for a late or main news bulletin that airs at, say, 10 pm. The first rough running order of stories to be covered is done at the morning meeting. What types of stories might this include?

- Breaking news
- Late news
- Running story
- Spot news i.e. instant, unforeseen, on the day event
- Diary piece i.e. planned
- Foreign or domestic
- Special area: business, arts, sport, science, crime, health, defence, social affairs, political.

How have these stories been found? Forward planning is the key, together with the production team keeping an eye on running stories, on the news wires and offerings from the news film agencies and other sources, reading the newspapers and coming up with suggestions to the news editor. With bi- and tri-media output there is, in the large news operations, a sharing of material and of journalists in the field or on location who could contribute to radio, TV and online. The newsgathering diaries are put together as a result of all the above. They are the blueprint for the news bulletin's official status as a 'record' of a nation's news or global events. Today in the era of multi-media and joint commissioning, all in the name of cost-cutting, the role of forward planners has become more important. They plan the movements for the Olympic Games, for example, for general elections, for EU summits and world conferences and then news is tied in to this and the cost of it. They also track the movements of foreign correspondents round the world and help ensure that as events unfold they can provide coverage for news. Planners liaise with news editors and executives. They don't work in isolation, because they have neither direct editorial control nor budgets of their own (apart from small amounts), so everything must be paid for by the newsgathering budgets. Also in rolling news stations and channels, the planners work closely with the daily producers so that enough material is brought in and delivered as and when the need increases as a story gathers momentum. For rolling or 24 hour news the teams producing segments of the programming take it in turns to plan, produce and package before their 'segment' goes on air. It is a news factory, keeping ahead by a few hours of what is on-air. It is also, of course, non-stop.

Planning and research

Where does information and material come from? The answer is from a number of different sources:

- Forward planning holds a diary of daily and future events
- Overnight and day planners are in constant contact with foreign correspondents and those already in the field covering stories to see what is on offer for a bulletin
- Press releases offer events and reports
- Press offices offer stories and people for interview as well as access and video
- Agencies offer pictures and feeds of material at certain times that intake editors oversee.

A good news bulletin contains a mix of stories that not only reflect events, but also keep the viewer 'entertained' by a good menu, with varied lengths of reports and types of items. Some reports of events are more suited to a breakfast or lunchtime audience, some for the evening slots. TV online websites provide a different mix too. The online print stories that often get the highest number of hits are those about animals or human interest or entertainment pieces, rather than hard news. Whatever the platform, the types of events that can arise remain the same. They are in these categories:

- Routine: press conferences, spokespeople for interview
- Disruptive: strikes, protests
- Direct access: new, sourced stories
- Accidents: oil spills, train crashes, floods, tsunamis
- Scandals: celebrity, political, exposés of child labour, sex trade, drug trafficking
- Serendipity: e.g. a siege, public grief over Princess Diana's death, the 9/11 attack on the World Trade Center, the 7/7 bombs in central London.

Newsgathering

No news editor comes to a bulletin empty-handed, there is always material that has arrived, is arriving and on offer; some of it detailed above comes from planning. Other material may have come in overnight or be offered via telephone calls or e-mails to the newsdesk. Packages that report stories, whether produced in the studio or from the field, both domestic and foreign, have to be decided upon. The top story or main story of the day is of primary importance: deciding how it can be reported, analysed, how it will develop or not, and who will cover it both from the newsdesk and from the reporting team.

Editorial controls

As with any business there are controls, both editorial and financial that determine what can be covered and the achievements of the news editor and team. They are:

- Editorial decisions – on the running order and importance of stories
- Time constraints – what can be achieved in time for the bulletin
- Financial and budget constraints – what can be afforded
- Geographic constraints – what can be brought in on time, or satellite links organised, if affordable
- Access – to a story, to people for interviews, to getting to locations in time
- Other source material, e.g. from agencies or independents or even a lack of pictures, that can help or hinder the proposed stories in the bulletin.

Selecting the stories for the running order is also determined by a number of things:

- What is on offer from bulletins already running
- Top news stories take priority

- Foreign stories if ready and accessible i.e. by satellite or courier
- Stand-by items
- Agency pictures often used as 'underlay'(or wallpaper), literally under the news presenter or a reporter's voice as commentary
- Independent footage on offer from individuals but more often from organisations e.g. Oxfam, UNICEF or Greenpeace.

Of course as the day goes on stories get dropped if a bigger breaking story comes in that demands priority, but if the reporter has been given the go-ahead the story might hold until the next day or a later bulletin.

The reporter's role is perhaps seen as the 'front of house' as she or he is seen on camera, but on a daily newsdesk the domestic reporter is the workhorse and it is certainly not all glamour, working maybe 10 or 12 hour shifts. Unlike VJs, the main bulletin reporters do not have to shoot or edit their reports. However, they too are always working against the clock, being sent off to places which are often difficult to get to, with a news crew or meeting a local cameraman, uncertain if they can get the story, if the weather will be against them, if traffic spoils the timing of it all and whether the story does deliver. The latter means that the facts were correct, that the interviews can be done and that the pictures are there.

The foreign correspondent or reporter sent into the field, when working with the bulletin – as opposed to delivering a cut story which has been pre-planned – is also under the pressure of time, needing to:

- Organise to cover the story as required
- Deliver it, via the internet, a webcam linked via the internet, a satellite phone linked to a portable dish, or fixed points in a studio or even via a phone line
- Liaise with the assignment or foreign editor on content which is not always easy via mobiles
- Update the story if it is a breaking one
- Be available for 'lives' or on camera to be interviewed by the studio presenter – this means being at a fixed point well ahead of the agreed 'cross' or 'two-way' into the bulletin.

'Roof monkeys' is one of the nicknames for those in the field who have to hover near the satellite feed point – often literally on a roof to broadcast live into a programme. At major global or national events you can see correspondents from the world's media standing in a line, facing the camera, waiting for their cue from the cameraman or the producer. It is not uncommon for a power failure to hit, as happened to me at one EU summit in Berlin, because everyone 'fired-up' at the same time and the strain on the city's electricity was too great. So all the preparation had to wait for the next hour or slot! Today, portable and literally fold-up dishes have made moving around much easier, so that the field correspondent is able to get on with what was traditionally his or her role as a reporter. That is to research, investigate, meet people, and find the locations and relevant shots to base a news report upon. The mobile or satellite phone of course helps keep everyone in touch, so that news and newswire updates and so on can be relayed to the reporter. The central newsdesk can see and assess a good deal more sometimes than the person in the field.

To return to our newsgathering process: the morning meeting has decided which stories to follow and everyone in the team works towards lining-up and assembling the contents.

The newsgathering day progresses

As the day goes on the reports start shaping up. There are a number of ways in which these are assembled; the cheapest and quickest are those produced in-house, that are either pre-recorded in the studio with graphics and some footage, or packaged in an edit suite using library or news agency footage and voiced by a reporter. Sometimes an interviewee is brought into the news centre to save the reporter having to travel, or recorded from a regional studio, or one at Westminster, for example, that is close to the House of Commons and House of Lords and useful for getting politicians. This interview is either sent 'live' down a booked feed line or if abroad, from a satellite link, or recorded and sent later. It can then be edited in an edit suite and packaged or added into a report. The presenter of a bulletin sometimes pre-records an interview or an item as if 'live' for inclusion in the bulletin. Other domestic stories can either be edited in regional newsrooms if a reporter is in the field and fed down the line, or brought back to the news centre base and cut in the edit suite.

Once done, a story is confirmed with the deputy news editor or assignment editor and given a mental tick in the running order for the bulletin as being there. The foreign story can similarly be on its way to be edited or packaged. The format of the reporter introducing a story and then throwing to what is called a 'donut', which is a previously prepared film, is now fairly standard practice. This allows for greater flexibility in the use of the film and also the reporter, who can appear pre-recorded for a bulletin or do a 'live' from a fixed point link and still introduce the film.

Editorial checks on the scripts and the pictures are made either if there is concern at the turn the story is taking or with the reporter, but in any case it is never broadcast without having been seen by usually two people, who act as 'gatekeepers'. One of the news producers is meanwhile preparing headline material taken from reports that will appear in the bulletin, or library or agency footage if the item is just a 'read' and nothing more. For example, a report that an airport was closed because of an unidentified object found on the runway that does not have any pictures, other than library ones of the airport, is a 'read'. The 'read' might be no longer than 10 seconds, or 30 words. All these items are being assembled to be used or discarded according to the final running order of the news programme. The assignment editor is working with a duty editor to ensure that stories are coming in and that the list of stories decided on in the morning meeting are being covered – also keeping an eye out for any new or breaking stories on the wires and from the agencies. Media managers record items as requested and as lines or feeds are set up. They are at the heart of the newsroom newsgathering operation both for TV and radio. They access the news 'traffic', as news material is called, as it comes in and download it for use by the programmes. News intake is a central internal network that allows all the news programmes to get access to all news items: agency material, satellite feeds etc., as well as to their own commissioned reports that come in from the field.

The newsgathering day continues

If this was an early evening bulletin, a second editorial meeting would take place at lunch-time to check on the progress of everything and talk about how the different items are shaping up. For bulletins going out at different times, there is still a series of meetings during their run-up to broadcast. This helps determine the items going into the bulletin as well as their slot or position in the running order. It is sometimes said that news values derive from assumptions or judgements about three things:

1   The audience: is it of interest and importance to the viewer and will it be enjoyed, understood and perceived as relevant?
2   Accessibility: prominence and ease of capture. The first point is obvious, whether the story is important and stays high on the priority list. And how easy it is to access by journalists, by use of which technology, the cost and time to achieve this.
3   Fit: can it fit in with the constraints of news production and the limitations of the medium? Does it make sense in terms of what is already known about the subject?

While all of this makes the newsroom and the process sound very controlled and organised, in fact the very nature of news means that – as one journalist put it – there are long periods of doing nothing and then all hell lets loose. A big story breaks and then the newsroom has to pull out all the stops, to redeploy people, maybe even call extra freelancers in, to report the story and get it ready for broadcast. Getting it on air, beating the competition, is the one aim to which the news team works. So are they controlled by it? Yes, because getting on air and getting it right on air are the imperatives. Sky News's motto is 'first with breaking news' but it often has to correct facts and figures, whereas the BBC does not broadcast unless facts have been checked. Sky, says that breaking the story is more important and that 'you heard it here first' wins them viewers.

Presentation

The presentation of a bulletin is determined by its pace. This is needed to keep the viewer interested, but also to cover the number of items within the bulletin. To vary the pace the items are arranged in order something like this: studio/package/live/package/and so on. (See the Appendix for an entire running order.) The bulletins have either one or two newscasters. The on-air team are portrayed as one big happy family throwing to each other – to the weather person, the business news person, the sports presenter and so on. All very polite, calling each other by their first names and thanking each other. Is this seen as reassuring for the viewer, or is it just the presentation culture that has developed to give some warmth and semblance of 'humanity' to what is after all an extremely artificial exercise? Certainly the newscasters are paid large salaries to be the 'face' of a bulletin, to give viewers the continuity and familiarity of seeing a regular presenter. Apart from the presenter, each bulletin is presented in its own house style. That is because it has identified through market research its core audience and so plays to its strengths. So the tone of the studio links is important, as is the language and style of the packages. The nature of television or broadcasting, even on broadband, is a more cumbersome and laborious process than that of producing a newspaper because of the logistics involved. The trend is for an increasing number of 'live' items where the news presenter throws to or has an exchange with a reporter in the field or in the studio for explanation, analysis or an update. This gives a greater sense of immediacy and also less need for packaged items which cost money and take up time, the things that the news editor and the team fight against. Watch any news bulletin and note down the different elements within it. See how many times they tell a story and then cross for an update from a reporter with the word 'LIVE' in the bottom or top corner of the screen. The reporter then usually re-affirms what the newscaster has just said, or what has appeared in a short previously prepared package or 'donut'. Repetition is now a common trend for rolling news – to fill in air-time.

There are changes in this traditional way of accessing news: for those going online, there is no studio, or presenter. You click on a headline to view a story, having read for yourself the headline and the introduction. Of course you choose which website to find your news on, but where it is coming from is no longer relevant, there is no news studio location. For local TV news it is the reverse and the local community know exactly where their news is coming from and identify with the presenters too as they see them often around their town and region. These viewers also seem keen to have something that reflects their lives and serves their needs, but for national and international news, they are still traditional in watching the main bulletins.

How the news is received

The way news is watched is changing, we all know that now, but the business of news remains: getting the facts right, pursuing accuracy, fairness and truth. It also has to entertain to keep its viewers. Of course there are biases, some of them determined by what can or cannot be sourced and reported in time – or at all. Then there is the bias of media ownership too that we will look at in a moment. There is the charge that journalists are becoming more interpretative, offering their opinions and analysis rather than just the facts. Watch any news bulletin to verify this for yourself. This is partly determined by viewers' demand for more insight into what events mean, but also it is a cheaper form of newsgathering, fewer pictures, fewer reports. It is interesting that surveys repeatedly show that the public views journalists with increasing scepticism and disbelief and yet they are being offered interpretations by them of how to view world events. An American joke is that 'There is currently an overabundance of news programming with supply easily outstripping demand'. The result in the US is a move away from hard news towards 'factotainment' that focuses on celebrity, entertainment and other areas like sport and the arts for its stories. This is in order to keep its audiences and so its advertising revenue.

Rolling news and 24-hour newsgathering

It's been called the 'CNN effect', because before CNN there were only set-time news bulletins. Suddenly there was 24 hours of news when CNN during the First Gulf War had 'live' coverage from its three reporters, Peter Arnett, John Holliman and Bernard Shaw, from the ninth floor room in the al-Rashid Hotel in Baghdad where they were trapped. It gave global audiences a feeling that they were hearing it, as it happened. Major networks took the CNN feeds so everyone heard the journalists as they pondered on what they could see from their hotel room. There were few pictures, just voiced reports. A new genre emerged helped by satellite technology. It was not 'new' journalism just faster, more continuous, less polished, and less edited. For some critics, the CNN effect was all too much.

> CNN types ... who make us experience the emptiness of TV as never before ... no one will hold this expert or general or that intellectual for hire to account for the idiocies and absurdities proffered the day before – since these will be erased by those the following day. In this manner everyone is amnestied by the ultra-rapid succession of phoney events and phoney discourses.
>
> (Jean Baudrillard, 1995)

CNN is now matched by BBC World, Al Jazeera International and viewers being able to access a whole range of channels offering news coverage from

Euronews to the major US networks, or MNet across Africa and of course within their own countries national or domestic stations. Although even these are accessible now via global satellites so that Sky and BBC's News24, for example, can be seen in Europe. However, when CNN ruled the roost as 'the' channel to watch, its perspective on world events rankled, especially in the Egyptian press where it was charged with bias.

Edward Said, a leading Arab journalist who died in 2003, railed against CNN, quoting an example of where he felt the bias lay. When reporting the death of King Hussein of Jordan, he felt that viewers were given the sense that they were present at an important Historical Occasion where something of Great Significance was unfolding before their very eyes. But, he said, 'its spin and interpretation of this man's life was essentially from a US viewpoint – on how he served the US peace process – and nothing to do with Jordan and his work within the Arab world'. Said's concern was that for many viewers, including those in the Arab world, CNN's broadcasts represented all that one needed to know about the world, reduced, packaged, and delivered without a trace of conflict or contradiction. He went so far as to call it a hijacking of the mind by a sophisticated apparatus whose purpose was deeply ideological. The kernel of this ideology is that 'we' define the world, state its purposes and meaning, control its unfolding history. In effect then, the funeral became the occasion for re-asserting control over a distant country, its people, history and departed monarch. And this seizure or hijacking permitted a whole series of further distortions which were later amplified by print journalism. (Said from *Al-Ahram Weekly*, Cairo, 18–24 February 1999, Issue No. 417)

So the subjects on which CNN spent many hours of coverage, for example, the Gulf War, Princess Diana's funeral, the Clinton impeachment, were elevated to the position of pre-eminence or importance possibly *out of proportion to their true news value*. This goes back to the need to fill airtime. Also the sway of the rolling news channels when they cover a main event for hours at a time. You believe in what they are saying because it sounds like the truth.

The concern of the Arab world in particular was answered by the creation of Al Jazeera, the Arabic channel that wanted to correct the bias of Western reporting. It has expanded now into Al Jazeera International, to ensure its message goes to the world, in English too. Their agenda is openly different, their top stories are the Palestine/Israeli conflict, Iraq, Afghanistan, Sudan and Arab events in the Middle East. They know their audience but they also know that they can determine their own agenda.

Single bulletin versus rolling news

The news production process outlined earlier in the chapter holds good for rolling news, but the content has through economic necessity become stretched until it is paper-thin. Repetition is a staple. The danger of immediate news is that accuracy can be at risk, although for Sky it does not always matter. Let us look at what does happen when checks are not made. An example is a report that went out in the US on the eve of the First Gulf War against Iraq. A story was circulating that Iraqis were throwing babies out of incubators and leaving them on the hospital floors to sell the incubators. A young woman weeping was interviewed telling the story. President Bush commented on it; everyone assumed it was true. Then it was revealed that the woman was in fact the Kuwaiti ambassador to the UN's daughter, and that she had been coached by the PR company Hill and Knowlton in telling the story because they were employed by the Free Kuwaiti movement, of which her father was a part. Moreover, none of it was true. What is the moral of this tale? For journalists to check their sources and double check. These principles still apply:

- A breaking piece of news has to be held until it can be checked
- Reliability and accuracy are more important than speed
- It is not enough just to interest the public
- You have to be trusted.

Another effect of going 'live' is that the same news is fed round the US, for example, and then globally, to keep costs down and also because the satellite technology is there. The result is a *single* version of events for a global audience, which ignores national differences and cultural values. Think back to Said's concern at the reporting of the death of King Hussein of Jordan. A major factor in favour of rolling news is that for the media owners 'live' is relatively cheap and can go on for hours without any editing.

Once it was proven that audiences were happy to watch for hours, a spin-off of 'live' became 'reality' television. It has revived TV ratings worldwide and is economic and cheaper to produce. In the US, shows like 'Fear Factor' cost little to produce – there are no actors to pay and no sets to maintain – and they get big ratings. Thus, American television has moved away from expensive sitcoms and on to cheap thrills. From 'Father Knows Best' to 'Who Wants to Marry My Dad?', and from 'My Three Sons' to 'My Big Fat Obnoxious Fiancé'. 'Big Brother' is perhaps the best-known show that began in the Netherlands, developed by Endemol, and now has been exported globally. John Humphrys, perhaps the most powerful news presenter in the UK, called 'reality' TV a tide of 'mind-numbing, witless vulgarity'. He sees it as a coarsening effect, turning 'human beings into freaks for us to gawp at'. And he sees it as damaging. No brow TV: no content, no nourishment, no good. Having said all of this Humphrys then appeared on a reality show himself, somewhat lessening his gravitas. However, the influence of 'live' is important because viewers are now accepting lower production standards, and a lower level of reporting and thus of journalism to go with it. The 2003 war in Iraq was viewed by many as a TV mini-series, because the embedded reporters with the troops on the frontline beamed 'live' into our homes. At the time there was no understanding of what these pictures meant in the context of the war. Then there was the siege of the school in Beslan in Chechnya. All we saw was chaos and confusion on camera. It was exciting, but it took the newspapers over the next two days to tell us the real story of what happened. There was no explanation about the Chechen situation or why these so-called terrorists were doing this. If there had been no satellite technology we would never have seen these pictures from Russia. TV news viewers used to expect the channels to report faithfully what has happened or is happening and to give it some context. When news has to roll continuously it still has to provide that and more; something that is not always happening, as we have seen.

Ways of watching TV

Understanding the news production process is important for anyone working or contributing to TV news, but also to any viewer who is watching the output. Realising that there is an agenda and learning how to 'read TV', means not taking it at screen value but standing back and thinking about how it is constructed, and *why* it is being presented to you, the viewer, in this way.

If any day of the week you picked up three different newspapers and read how each reported the top story you would begin to see that they all write about an event in a different way, from the headline to the words. Why do they do this? Well, papers are owned by different people and their politics are represented in the way the news is presented and interpreted. The same applies to broadcasting. So if you stand back and think about what you are being told then you are not a passive consumer, you are judging what matters to you. That is the basis for being a journalist, to care about things and to reflect that in your work. Philip Roth, the author, described the difference between being a novelist in the West and in the Soviet Union, behind what was then known as the Iron Curtain. 'In Eastern Europe nothing is permitted and everything matters; with us everything is permitted but nothing matters'.

This applies to the news business: the more information we have, the less significant it becomes. Look at it a different way. If you have one pair of shoes they are so important; if you have 50 they are of less importance. But more than that, what matters is what affects you personally. A car accident you have matters; a multi-car pile-up on the road matters less because you were not involved except as a recipient of the news.

So what matters to you? You are watching TV and you want to see reports that tell you what has happened but you also need to think about how it is being presented to you.

As an exercise, read the list below and then use it to watch a bulletin yourself so that you understand. Look at the structure of a news bulletin.

- Opening music – important sounding.
- Titles – animated graphics use hard lines, not soft curves. The BBC had to replace one set of titles when viewers complained that they were too 'fascist' in design.

- Set – the news studio, streamlined, uncluttered. A big screen for presenters sometimes to stand in front of. It appears to emphasise the importance of pictures over the newscaster, but is just a new studio 'feature' that in the UK news broadcasters have now adopted.
- The newscaster – usually attractive and well-presented. Must be a credible and believable person. They used to be people with an air of authority or knowing, but are now often young men and women employed more for their looks and if they are journalists it is rarely obvious. They appear as mouthpieces, reading the news and asking prepared questions of correspondents and others.
- Opening headlines – there to hook you, showing you the menu of what you'll be seeing. This is usually pre-recorded before the bulletin begins, to get the timing of the voice to the short-cut picture menu right.

Then the bulletin begins with a mixture of reads, two-way 'live' crosses and reports.

If there is a commercial break, just before it comes up there is a 'bumper' showing you what is coming up next. This is accompanied by the words, 'so stay with us' or 'bye for now'. The family of presenters includes co-anchor, regional newscaster, business news presenter, sports commentator and weather person. Everyone is on first name terms – all thanking each other as they pass to each other. It is all timed to move fast to keep the viewer interested or at least watching. Repetition of the headlines at the end of the bulletin is a convention, a reiteration or re-enforcement of the stories considered the main news by the broadcaster.

Other points to consider are:

- TV is not what happened, but what someone has decided is worth reporting
- TV news = a show = a commodity
- TV attracts viewers = ratings = licence to broadcast = higher advertising rates = profit for owners to plough back or take
- You consume it; here today, gone tomorrow.

Later in the day you can watch the news and it has changed. The 'latest' news is what you are supposed to crave. Watching the news can be an addiction – because it is meant to be. You should know who owns the channels you are watching and what their politics are.

Why? Because this is how the news food chain works:

- Investors/owners
- Parent company
- Media company/advertisers
- News department
- Journalists
- Audience.

So let us learn more about media owners. Global news channels are owned, apart from the state-funded ones like the BBC, SABC, PBS, and FR1, by individuals: Rupert Murdoch, Michael Bloomberg, and Silvio Berlusconi, for example, in Italy. Other channels are owned by corporations: CNN (Time Warner, but before that Ted Turner), Fox News (Murdoch owned), Sky News (Murdoch), CNBC business news (part of NBC owned by General Electric), Bloomberg Business channel (owned by Michael Bloomberg, present mayor of New York City), Al Jazeera funded by the Emir of Qatar. It is the owners who 'through their wealth, determine the style of journalism we get' (Michael Foley). As Rupert Murdoch put it so eloquently, 'I did not come all this way *not* to interfere.' The Murdoch News Corporation which owns Sky News and Fox News is clear about influencing the news that itput out. This is what executive spokespeople told two journalists who lost their jobs after refusing to alter their stories: 'We paid $3 billion for these TV stations. We will decide what news is.' One foreign correspondent, Sam Kiley, resigned from his Middle East post when his reports on the Arab/ Israeli conflict had to be changed in line with the perceived view of the proprietor, one R. Murdoch.

> Murdoch's executives were so scared of irritating him that when I pulled off a scoop by tracking, interviewing and photographing the unit in the Israeli army which had killed Mohammed al-Durrah, the 12-year-old boy whose death was captured on film and became the iconic image of the conflict, I was asked to file the piece *'without mentioning the dead kid'*. After that conversation I was left wordless, so I quit'.
>
> (Sam Kiley, 2001)

Murdoch's most recent 24-hour cable news channel, Fox, launched in 1996 and has become his most controversial. Fox News is now the most watched channel in the US beating CNN into second place. When it comes to Fox News Channel, conservatives do not feel the need to 'work the ref' because he is already on their side. Fox is openly conservative, siding with the Republicans. It is part of the network of fiercely partisan outlets such as the *Washington Times*, the *Wall Street Journal* and conservative radio talk shows like Rush Limbaugh. Together they write and broadcast material that is effectively right-wing. Yet, at the same time, the network bristles at the slightest suggestion of a conservative tilt. 'I challenge anybody to show me an example of bias in Fox News Channel' (Rupert Murdoch, *Salon*, 3/1/01). Fox News Channel is 'not a conservative network!' says chairman Roger Ailes. 'I absolutely, totally deny it. The fact is that Rupert [Murdoch] and I, and by the way, the vast majority of the American people, believe that most of the news tilts to the left.' Fox's mission is 'to provide a little more balance to the news' and 'to go cover some stories that the mainstream media won't cover'. The channel has slogans like 'Fair and balanced' and 'We report, you decide'. It also during the Iraq War of 2003 sent the controversial figure of former Colonel Oliver North to report as an embed with the troops. North's presentations were patriotic in their language and perspective. He would start his reports with comments like 'It's a wonderful day here ...'. Fox took seriously President Bush's threat to journalists 'you're either with us or against us'. In 1996, Andrew Kirtzman, a respected New York City cable news reporter, was interviewed for a job with Fox and says that the managers wanted to know what his political affiliation was. 'They were afraid I was a Democrat,' he told the *Village Voice* (10/15/96). When Kirtzman refused to give his party ID, 'all employment discussion ended', according to the *Voice*.

Then there is Italy's businessman and politician, Silvio Berlusconi. When he was Prime Minister and Italy's richest man, with major media holdings, he was quite naturally asked about a potential conflict of interests. His reply: 'If I, taking care of everyone's interests, also take care of my own, you can't talk about a conflict of interest.' Berlusconi was forced to resign as Prime Minister on 2 May 2006. In the run-up to Italian elections in the month before he stepped down, one of the most controversial aspects of the campaign was the media coverage. For Mr Berlusconi's investment company Fininvest controls Italy's three biggest private television stations. The Berlusconi family has ownership of around 96 per cent of Fininvest. Fininvest has a 48.6 per cent controlling stake (worth around £3 billion) in Mediaset, the terrestrial television group that competes with state-owned RAI and operates three networks: Canale 5, Italia 1 and Retequattro. And his appointees run the public ones. Opponents complained that an Italian voter could not escape blanket coverage favourable to Mr Berlusconi. They said his control of the media extended beyond the news agenda, and that comedians who lampooned the Prime Minister never appeared on TV again. Some 82 per cent of Italians depend only on television for news, the highest percentage in the EU and the news they are getting is usually from a Berlusconi controlled channel. Fininvest also has a controlling stake in Mondadori, Italy's largest book and magazine publishing group with 30 per cent position in the domestic book market and 38 per cent in the magazine market respectively. Fininvest controls *Il Giornale*, a leading national newspaper that competes with L'Espresso's *La Repubblica* and with *La Stampa* and *Corriere della Sera* of the RCS group. It has a 36 per cent stake in financial-services group Mediolanum. Other holdings include property, multimedia, printing and telephone directories. There have been recurrent moves to force Berlusconi to divest some of his media assets – and he has made undertakings to that effect – but there is apparently little action. On 19 January 2002 the *Economist* magazine commented that:

> Mr Berlusconi has yet to remove the ubiquitous conflicts between his private and public concerns. Because his companies are embroiled in almost every part of the economy, his failure to do so casts doubts on the motives behind so many of his projects, whatever their merits.

Following 9/11 and the attack on the World Trade Center in New York, the media put the Arab world, the search for Osama Bin Laden and all the subsequent stories high on their agendas. For the Arab world their interpretation of events was biased and incorrect. As a result the Al Jazeera channel, meaning 'the peninsula' or 'island' in Arabic, was launched. It is the largest Arabic news channel in the Middle East that established itself globally after being sent and then showing exclusive video tapes of Osama Bin Laden talking. It has a clearly stated agenda, seeking to redress the balance of how the Arab world is represented in the Western media, especially the United States. To counteract what it sees as Western censoring of what is shown on the news, especially during the Iraq War of 2003, Al Jazeera declared that it would portray 'the ugly face of war'. This has brought with it myriad problems and a backlash from countries that see the station as promoting terrorism in general and Al Qaeda in particular.

Al Jazeera's origins date back to 1995 when the BBC, which had built a strong Arabic-language news service through its World Service radio network, signed a deal with the Saudi owned company Orbit Communications to provide Arabic newscasts for Orbit's main Middle East channel. However, the BBC's insistence on editorial independence clashed with the Saudi government's unwillingness to permit reporting on controversial issues, such as a documentary showing graphic executions and the activities of prominent Saudi dissidents. In April 1996, when the BBC broadcast a story on human rights in the Saudi Kingdom which showed footage of the beheading of a criminal, Orbit pulled out of the deal and the station closed down. A few months later, Sheik Hamad, the Emir of Qatar, agreed to fund Al-Jazeera and for them to 'report the news as they see it'. 'I believe criticism can be a good thing', the Emir said in a 1997 speech, 'and some discomfort for government officials is a small price to pay for this new freedom'. The initial set-up costs were $150 million. The station hoped to become self-sufficient through advertising by 2001, but when this failed to occur, the Emir agreed to continue subsidising it. To the West and especially the US, the channel is seen as a 'terrorist organisation' (Bill O'Reilly). Concerned about the anti-American stance, the US government funded the Arabic-language satellite TV station Al Hurra in 2004. The word means 'the free one', and is based in Virginia, financed by Congress, and beamed across the Arab world. Dubbed the 'American answer to Al Jazeera', *The Washington Post* newspaper described Al Hurra as 'the U.S. government's largest and most expensive effort to sway foreign opinion over the airwaves since the creation of Voice of America in 1942'. Programming consists of two daily hour-long newscasts, and sports, cooking, fashion, technology and entertainment programmes, political talk shows and magazine-type news programmes. It has bureaus in Amman, Baghdad, Beirut and Dubai. It is not often quoted for its output.

Al Jazeera's aggression has met with political action by countries. For example, the Bahrain Information Minister Nabeel Yacoob Al Hamer banned

Al Jazeera correspondents from reporting from inside the country on 10 May 2002, saying that the station was biased towards Israel and against Bahrain. It lifted the ban in 2004. Al Jazeera reporter Taysir Allouni was arrested in Spain on 5 September 2003, on a charge of having provided support for members of Al Qaeda. Although he pleaded not guilty of all the charges against him, Allouni was sentenced on 26 September to seven years in prison for being a financial courier for Al Qaeda. Allouni insists he is a journalist who was doing his job by interviewing Bin Laden after the 11 September attack on the United States. Al Jazeera cameraman Sami Al Hajj was detained while in transit to Afghanistan as an 'enemy combatant' in December 2001, and is now held without charge in Guantanamo Bay. Despite all these moves against their reporters and staff, Al Jazeera has not pulled back from its original position of wanting to show things how they are. During the Iraq War in 2004, Al Jazeera broadcast several video tapes of various kidnapping victims which had been sent to the network. The videos were filmed by the groups after kidnapping a hostage. The hostages are shown, often blindfolded, pleading for their release. Al Jazeera says it has attempted to help secure the release of kidnapping victims, and also broadcast pleas from family members and government officials. Contrary to some allegations, including the oft-reported comments of Donald Rumsfeld on 4 June 2005, Al Jazeera has never shown beheadings which often appear on internet websites. The US continues to argue about how Al Jazeera reports the Israel-Palestinian conflict. Its vocabulary differs from the West, calling 'suicide bombers', 'martyrs'. The Al Jazeera explanation is clear:

> We figure that if somebody dies in the cause of defending his own land then he is a martyr, but if he carries a bomb into Tel Aviv and blows himself up, then he is not a martyr.
>
> (Jihad Ballout, Communications Director)

Al Jazeera says it has had a liberalising effect on Arab countries and the estimated 30–50 million viewers it has worldwide. Its international English language news channel, launched in December 2006, is an attempt to capture a wider audience but also to have its brand of broadcasting understood by English language viewers. Its future, reliant on grants, plus advertising revenue and sales from footage like the Bin Laden tapes which cost $20,000 per minute to purchase, is assured. Al Jazeera's potential dominance of the Middle Eastern markets resulted in 2006 with the BBC re-launching its Arabic TV service, based in Cairo and filling what they perceive as a gap in the broadcasting to the Middle East. Another group of Saudi investors encouraged enough by Al Jazeera's relative success, launched Al Arabiya in 2003. It has managed to create an impact, partly as a balance to Al Jazeera, and covers all the Middle East, Asia Pacific, South East Asia, North Africa, Europe, the Americas and Australia. It broadcasts hourly news bulletins, 24 hours a day. Al Jazeera has shaken up global broadcasting at a time in history when the world has been focussed on the Arab world, without understanding or making sense of its perspectives.

Another international 24-hour news and information channel broadcasting around the world from its base at BBC Television Centre in London is BBC World. It is commercially funded but an integral part of the BBC's commitment to global broadcasting and, along with BBC World Service Radio, aims to attract viewers who wish to keep ahead of global news events. BBC World's motto is 'to keeps its viewers not just informed, but well informed, with in-depth analysis and cutting edge interviews, the story from all sides'. BBC World, under the original name of BBC World Service Television, was set up in 1991 to serve Asia and the Middle East. It rapidly expanded through the launch of new satellites. As they went up, so the BBC (along with CNBC, Sky, Bloomberg and others) could expand into new territories e.g. on Multichoice in South Africa. Trading on its alma mater, with one of the best-known brands in the world (along with Coca Cola, Nike and Microsoft), BBC World has the same BBC editorial guidelines: to deliver impartial and objective journalism of the highest standard. It also has a crucial union agreement for its correspondents and 'stringers' (non-staff journalists on a retainer or contract deal) worldwide to use video cameras. This allows for increased coverage of events at an economic rate.

Returning to our ownership theme, it is apparent that channels, when successful, exert a good deal of influence over world events and how people consider them. So the answer to the question of why do media moguls like Murdoch and Berlusconi want to own news channels or newspapers is quite simply power. Before television, the newspaper magnates were, like Rupert Murdoch today, clear about their motives for ownership.

'Merely for the purpose of making propaganda with no other motive' said Lord Beaverbrook, press magnate in 1949. Owning a newspaper or a TV news station gives them a voice, or as Robert Maxwell owner of the British *Daily Mirror* in the 1980s (amongst other publications) said, 'a personal megaphone'.

So what are the news content determinants? How is the news shaped and defined? The list that follows is examined point by point:

- Agenda of the owners
- Financial pressures
- Commercial pressures/advertising
- Political pressures – for national and state-funded stations.

Agenda of the owners

On the agenda are the rewards for being high-profile media moguls. These come in the form of knighthoods, invitations to political and social events (especially if money is given to the political parties), maybe diplomatic postings in the US, but above all power and control. Wealth buys these same moguls football or baseball teams that are also part of the public entertainment sphere. Murdoch for one has turned this into a money-spinner with his sports channels bidding and getting sports rights to the world's top events so that viewers are forced to subscribe to watch the cricket or rugby that they follow. His most recent acquisition though, as discussed in Chapter 7, is that of MySpace.com.

The accepted equation is that news = discussion = public opinion. It can be influential and that is what the media owners are after. How does this happen? People talk about the news to each other and repeat it, pass it on. Once it is being discussed the question is, does it remain news or turn into public opinion? For example, the story about weapons of mass destruction, WMD, began as a news item. Saddam Hussein, it was stated on the news, had WMD, according to President Bush and UK Prime Minister Blair. So, they told their countries and the world, they felt it right to invade Iraq. The debate then developed about what WMD are, do they exist, was there any evidence of them existing and if so what kind of damage can they do.

The UN weapons inspectors sent in by an enquiring world could not find them, doubt was cast upon their existence, but war was declared anyway. This in turn caused the largest anti-war demonstrations in the streets of London, Washington and Europe protesting about going to war without being sure of the facts. 'Not in our name', the banners proclaimed. And even post-war, the WMD issue did not go away. It had changed into something much bigger than a news piece, had become a public and global debate that stayed in the news. Politically Bush and Blair survived even when it was discovered that there were no WMD.

Saddam Hussein has now been hanged.

Of course a running story like this is manna from heaven for any media organisation, to keep their audience interested and hooked. One theory is that the media are usurping parliament, where a nation's issues are debated, by becoming the forum for national debate. Campaigns carried out in the newspapers are then picked up by TV news. Why campaign? Well it makes people buy newspapers and watch TV – which is what the media want. War is another viewer-puller and the second Iraq war became a long-running mini-series as cameramen and reporters embedded with the army sent back live pictures. Viewing figures were extremely high for this period.

Financial pressures on owners

However, from the media owners' point of view covering a war is a financial pressure because news programmes have to cover major events, whatever the cost. Wars are expensive; satellite and digital technology have reduced costs and provided access but it is still expensive; 'live' news is cheaper but rolling news requires more staff and more facilities.

News anyway is costly because:

- At any one time there are some sixty conflicts worldwide
- Special events, disasters, political elections, ceremonials are compulsory to cover but can prove expensive
- Global sports like the World Cup, Formula One motor-racing, the Olympics and so on are also costly whether buying rights, or getting satellite feed time and bookings
- Global link-ups are expected for global news and it is more costly than national or even continental news coverage.

Commercial pressures

In order to maintain their positions, of course, media owners and conglomerates need to make money and to satisfy their investors and shareholders. Investors expect some sort of influence or prestige attached to their investment in an organisation that broadcasts news. Media moguls are under commercial pressures from advertisers, the traditional supporters of media, to produce the programmes that attract high viewing figures. The equation works like this: News bulletins = Audiences = Advertisers = Money for Media owners. Owners need to make money and because news gets an audience, they can sell the high ratings, for example, 40 million people watch the nightly news in the US, to advertisers.

For commercial channels a reliance on advertising as the only source of direct funding is well established. Advertisers on the US main news networks, NBC, CBS, ABC and Fox spend around £3 billion per annum. Advertisers pay for the audience that the media firm delivers based on independent research. This shows what the audience is: their wealth or economic status, if they are home-owners, family size and so on. Traditionally the higher the income bracket, the more the advertisers have to pay and are happy to pay in order to reach the so-called As and Bs that they feel will become expensive product buyers. This has now changed with reality shows where the audience is wider spread, but also the twenty years or so of consumer power and the global preoccupation with shopping now delivers a wider variety of incomes and statuses. (The internet is now attracting advertisers away from broadcast TV in growing numbers.) American consumer research shows advertisers like news programmes, taking advertising spots before between and after news programmes. It is believed that consumers or viewers believe in the news that they are watching and that this credibility factor leaks over into the adverts for products that they watch. The advertisers, for example, in New York watch the Nielsen ratings published in the *New York Times* weekly. They watch the audience size and vary their product placements accordingly. It has become a straitjacket for the media owners and broadcasters, to maintain their audience share and so their profits. In the UK, JICTAR viewing figures are published weekly and they too affect a broadcaster's advertising earnings. This relationship with advertisers has been blamed for the so-called dumbing-down of TV content. If Big Brother attracts audiences, say, of over 9 million viewers, then advertisers are happy and so they put on pressure for the show to continue, ignoring its content. These programmes are then hyped in the newspapers that jump on the bandwagon, getting lots of column content and guaranteed to attract people to buy their papers.

Commercial pressures also mean that consolidation is inevitable, as profit margins are squeezed. In the United States a situation has now developed where, according to one of the former independents, Ted Turner, founder of CNN (which is now part of Time Warner group), it has gone too far. Virtually all competition has been either bought up or found it cannot survive. Turner's current battle is that he is too small a fish in the media pond and that the US government or rather the FCC, Federal Communications Commission, is allowing too great a consolidation.

'That's why', he says, 'we haven't seen a new generation of people like me or even Rupert Murdoch – independent television upstarts who challenge the big boys and force the whole industry to compete and change'.

Today, media companies are more concentrated than at any time over the past 40 years.

The media giants now own not only broadcast networks and local stations but also the cable companies that pipe in the signals of their competitors and the studios that produce most of the programming. For example, in 1990 the major broadcast networks, ABC, CBS, NBC and Fox, fully or partially owned just 12.5 per cent of the new series they aired. By 2000, it was 56.3 per cent. Just two years later, it had surged to 77.5 per cent. Large corporations are more profit-focused and risk-averse. They often kill local programming because it is expensive, and they push national programming because it is cheap, even if their decisions run counter to local interests and community values.

An example of this was in 2002, when a freight train derailed near Minot, North Dakota, in the US, releasing a cloud of dangerous anhydrous ammonia over the town. The police tried to call local radio stations, six of which are owned by radio giant Clear Channel Communications. According to news reports, it took them over an hour to reach anyone as no one was answering the Clear Channel phone. By the next day 300 people had been hospitalised, many partially blinded by the ammonia. Pets and livestock died. Through all this, oblivious to events, Clear Channel continued beaming its programming from its headquarters in San Antonio, Texas, some 1,600 miles away.

The example proves that consolidation can mean a decline in the local focus of both news and programming. After analysing 23,000 stories on 172 news programmes over five years, the Project for Excellence in Journalism found that big media news organisations relied more on syndicated feeds and were more likely to air national stories with no local connection. Of course this is all good news for the community and local TV broadband and cable channels that are mushrooming.

Today, the only way for media companies to survive is to own everything up and down the media chain. From broadcast and cable networks to the sitcoms, movies, and news broadcasts you see on those stations; to the production studios that make them; to the cable, satellite, and broadcast systems that bring the programmes to your television set; to the websites you visit to read about those programmes; to the way you log on to the internet to view those pages. Big media today wants to own the party: the glasses, the drink, the DJ, the music (the copyright if possible no doubt), the nightclub, as well as the building it is in.

Ninety per cent of the top 50 US cable TV stations are owned by the same parent companies that own the broadcast networks. Yes, Disney's ABC network has at the last count lost viewers to cable networks. But it is losing viewers to cable networks like its own ESPN, ESPN2, and The Disney Channel!

The situation in the UK is that while in both digital radio and digital television advances in technology are facilitating the entry of new market participants, the Communications Act 2003 allowed for more consolidation to take place in broadcasting, particularly in the television sector. The Carlton and Granada merger, long awaited by the financial City institutions and stock exchange, came to fruition in February 2004 with the formation of ITV plc. This brought together all English and Welsh ITV licences, with the aim of creating a force able to compete effectively with the BBC and BSkyB (of which Sky News is a part, within the Murdoch empire). The new entity planned to save £100 million (representing around 5 per cent of its cost base) at the expense of regional job losses. To prevent abuse of its dominant position in advertising air-time sales, ITV plc agreed not to increase prices unless audiences also rose.

In May 2004, ITV agreed a deal to acquire SMG's 25 per cent stake in GMTV, an independent commercial UK channel (making it the majority shareholder). BSkyB in November 2006 bought a 17.9 per cent stake in ITV, making them the largest shareholder so that if anyone like the German broadcaster RTL or even cable operator NTL bid for ITN, BSkyB would have a say. UK Channels Four and Five have announced that they are looking at the possible benefits of merging. In the cable sector the merger between NTL:Telewest and Virgin Mobile in July 2006 added another resource to the cable business's portfolio.

Political pressures

State broadcasters are also under pressures and constraints, but these are different from those of the commercial channels, apart from the need to keep viewers. In the UK, the publicly-funded licence fee supports the BBC. The BBC operates under the terms of a Royal Charter. In order to get a renewal and an increase in the TV licence fee that covers the costs of its broadcasting, it has the job of periodically defending its spending to government (as opposed to a Board of Directors and shareholders) and providing evidence that it is acting according to its Charter and editorial guidelines. So it has to maintain and improve the quality and reach of its news programming, for example, without increasing costs. It has, unlike a commercial organisation, no overdraft facility and no owner to bail it out. To launch its rolling News24 channel, for example, it has had to ensure sharing of content with other news bulletins and to cut costs by reduction in staff.

Conclusion

So what is the impact of all these considerations, of cost, advertising and political pressures on programming? It can be seen in programming, as a whole and in news in particular.

In the UK, as in the US and Europe, television channels are increasingly under pressure to keep and win audiences, as the television market fragments. More people are watching news and programming via the internet that means that advertisers, the long-time funders of ITV for one, are now looking to the internet too. They are trying out viral ads and placing ads or sponsorship on favourite sites like MySpace, this despite mainstream programmes on linear TV still attracting high audiences and protesting that TV is not going away just yet. Communications convergence that has been written about and forecast is now a reality, albeit in a different form. When people talked of convergence in the 1990s, they foresaw a world where the computer, telephone, television and radio became a single device in the home. In practice, the number of devices has proliferated while content, often re-versioned and shortened, is becoming available on a wide range of platforms. Mobiles and other hand-held devices are becoming capable of receiving services from different platforms. The new media revolution is discussed at length in Chapter 7.

Understanding the constraints under which news is produced, as discussed in this chapter, should be helpful in seeing what part they play in your life as a viewer, if nothing else. Knowing who owns what, how channels are run and the media owners' position, helps put in perspective the news as you watch it. It would help if a news programme opened with information about who owns it, how they vote, who the shareholders are and so on, because it tells you straightaway what might be influencing the news you are watching. You assume it to be straight reporting of the facts and events as they have happened. Why is TV news important to think about? It is an integral and defining part of our culture.

We need news and if we had no TV or radio, we would still be driven by a need to find out what was happening and go out into the streets to find ways of getting information. It is human nature. Not knowing is now scary. Knowing makes us feel secure in terms of where we are.

So if you become a VJ or broadcast journalist you are expected to know about the different organisations. If you go to work for Sky or CNN or the BBC, ITV, CNBC, Bloomberg or Al Jazeera, you should know about that company and its politics and policies. In the following chapter we look at filming techniques and how to produce reports for the news by VJs.

Questions to students

1   What can you remember about a news bulletin once it is finished?
2   Why are we, the viewers and listeners, hooked now on this concept of 'live'?
3   Is it important to understand media ownership?
4   Analyse any news bulletin and see how many elements there are and time them to see how long they are.
5   Can news stimulate political action? Can it bring about new laws and changes in the existing laws? Think of appalling crimes against children where parents and others have lobbied for change.

6 Filming for new and old media

This chapter looks at how to film and produce reports, for would-be VJs, those already practising and journalists wanting to develop video skills. The market and opportunities for videojournalism are opening up at an unprecedented rate, so from a career perspective, having VJ skills, i.e. being able to shoot, write and edit, are undoubtedly 'must-haves' for anyone going into the communications business. Kinsey Wilson, editor-in-chief of USAToday.com, the website of the biggest selling daily nationwide, forecast in 2006 the top trend to watch on newspaper sites would be 'the continued, expanded use of video and real experimentation around how video is best deployed on the internet'. How right she was.

What does this all mean? Well for anyone looking to be employed as a journalist, it means that multi-skilling is going shortly to become a requisite. Moreover it is not just for newspaper sites or local TV, but also for the dedicated internet broadcast channels that are springing up offering all sorts of video content. They have emerged because the technology is now simpler for companies to do this, but they are also following the success of video blogs or vlogs, and the immensely popular MySpace and YouTube, Bebo, OhMyNews, Current TV, Flickr, Google Video, and Yahoo! where you can upload your videos. Why are these so popular? Well as more people are using video to express their views and to film material, they want to share it and it appears there is an audience who wants to watch, surf and comment on their offerings. You can sell your video too. It is 'our' space that can compete with traditional or conventional broadcasting and is subject to few guidelines.

With VJ skills you can shoot not just for broadcast but for corporate webcasts and video streaming online, offer user-generated content (UGC,) and make vlogs and mobcasts to mobile phones. There are companies now specialising in mobile content that need people with video skills and every newspaper or company or broadcaster that wants to put video on their website needs those skills too. Even the PR industry is finding that without internet communication tools in their kit, they are lagging behind and so are their clients.

Can anyone become a VJ?

This is a debate that centres on the idea that some skills are innate and cannot be taught, so that some people have an 'eye' for a shot and a 'nose' for a good story and that it cannot be learnt. This the view of one practising VJ, Gareth Jones:

> I believe VJing is not for everyone and that therefore it is impossible to bring in across the board. Broadcasting is an increasingly fast and complex tri-media activity. New editing technology means VJs can now do desk-top editing; journalists are being trained in how to input their words and pictures directly into their news websites. We are now asking more of journalists than ever before in terms of multi-skilling and not everyone can or should become skilled in *all* these disciplines. Apart from anything else, I don't think all journalists can get all the practice time they need in *all* these new skills in order to get fast, proficient and confident. I think the best newsrooms will have combinations and permutations of these skills: there'll be VJs who can edit, but there'll also be people who may just specialise in writing and processing words and pix for TV and online. Online is demanding people who can write well and who specialise in subjects (BSkyB have just appointed a bunch of such specialists). But I'd also like to think there'll be VJs who are valued for their ability to be street-wise, able to deal with the difficulties of gathering material in the big wide world. I find that broadcast journalism risks becoming increasingly newsroom-bound. There aren't enough people with practical newsgathering skills developed on the street or in the field. VJs are often part of that culture and need to be nurtured and appreciated for that.

Can print journalists make video reports too, without special training?

As newspapers shift into multi-media mode their journalists are being asked when out on a story to use video cameras too. While special courses are being run to help journalists think visually, the same principles of story-telling remain. However, combining words and pictures means inverting your priorities. The pictures lead on a video report, but the facts of the story and its content still dictate what those pictures are. So you can have the same interviewees, for example, but for the pictures you have to introduce them and then place, frame and film them in a relevant and acceptable light. Or if you're covering an accident, say, you will note for the print piece the scene and describe it: twisted and damaged cars, an overturned lorry, an ambulance ferrying the three people hurt; but for the video you have to show all this and use the language of filming. The wide shot, the close-ups, some action of the ambulance arriving or leaving and so on. The advice and ideas that follow in this chapter will help set you thinking about these skills.

So what should you bring to being a VJ or practising videojournalism? A short checklist of key skills includes:

- an ability to engage with people
- an inquiring mind so as to ask pertinent questions
- a visual awareness, to combine pictures with words and a storyline
- a value system and objective view of the order of things, plus a sense of moral, ethical and legal issues that might affect recording video.

The rest of the chapter is going to cover the following topics:

- *identifying a story* from various sources and for its relevance
- *researching* and how you can do this
- *pitching a story* on the basis of your further research
- *structuring and writing* out a rough draft or running order
- *sourcing other material* like graphics, extra footage from the tape library or other sources if you are sure of your storyline and needs.

In the filming section there is advice on:

- *film techniques* and using the right shots
- *logging your shots* to find the best soundbites, shots and takes on the piece to camera (if there is one); this can be in a rough form as you download and choose shots, but it helps to have a record
- *scripting* using recorded material as the basis of the report
- *editing* often done as you script, but easier to cut to your already written script and quicker.

Beyond these are the new media skills that are more technical but nonetheless a key part of the videojournalism craft, like uploading or sending a report that you have edited on your pc or laptop, to get it on air or onto a website.

Identifying a story

What *is* a story? A story is when something out of the ordinary happens. That then becomes news. For example: a ferry capsizing, a plane crash, a new law coming into force, a birth, a death, an election, or an uprising. Events where people win, lose, commit crimes or stop crimes. Anything you can think of that 'happens'. It only becomes news if it is reported, either by word of mouth, electronically or usually if it appears in the media. Most TV news stories are started by an alert of some kind, via a news agency wire, a newspaper piece, an internet RSS feed alert, a contact or a traditional press release or e-release.

As a journalist your role is to identify how strong or good a story is, whether it is one you have been given in the news room or found yourself, or been told about. Does it answer the key questions, the so what and why does it matter?

To gauge how important or relevant it is ask if it addresses these questions:

- Is it new?
- Is it a new twist on an old tale?
- Does it affect people other than those featured – i.e. is it of wider significance?
- Will it affect people?
- Would it help people to have this information?
- Is it relevant to your audience?
- Is it an eyebrow raiser?

Someone has described defining a news story as being like 'nailing jelly to a wall'. It keeps slipping away or changing or not being quite what it appeared to be. For example, a flood is reported to have drowned 50 people, but on checking it is cattle not people; a crime wave turns out to be two burglaries in a town not 200. The only way to pin a story down is to research it further and without doing this, a journalist is unable to progress. If you do not know the answers, you cannot pitch it at a news conference to a news editor or get on with your job. Research = investigation and although there are investigative journalists who research long-term stories or documentaries, every journalist has to be a detective. Everyone has to inquire about facts and the sequence of events.

Daily news by its very nature can be seen as a recipe demanding 'just add water' reporting, rather than 'first marinade the meat for 3 days'.

Interestingly the public in general disapprove of journalists but approve of the practice of uncovering and reporting on corruption and fraud in business, in government and other organisations. Think back to the WMD story discussed in the previous chapter. It got the headlines and almost brought down the UK government, or at least the Prime Minister Tony Blair when it turned out he had lied about the presence of these weapons. The WMD media campaign got the public involved, as do famine reporting and general disaster reporting, where raising awareness is responded to by donations of money or concerts for charities. Today more reporting is aware of the public's wish to be involved; it is seen by the level of interaction online and the response even to TV news appeals for mobile phone footage of the 7 July bomb damage in London in 2005. Why do the public want to be involved? Part of the answer is that they now can, without having to a write a letter and post it or even call a news desk or switchboard. Knowing this makes a journalist's job in many respects easier. The 'field' is no longer a hostile zone where people are unhelpful and where filming is a problem. Probably the contrary.

The rules by which the journalist works, however, do not change. Your responsibility is to not only be sure of your facts but doubly so, as what you report could lead to people losing their jobs, a change in public opinion, a business reputation being lost or a political career being left in shreds.

Think again of the WMD story. The 'letting drop' of the scientist's name, David Kelly, who had said there were no WMD and had met with journalists including Andrew Gilligan, led him to take his life. While this was a complicated and complex situation where it was the government who gave the media heavy hints about who Kelly was, Gilligan did have to admit his source for his story. Did he or anyone else know the fatal consequences of this? Even with hindsight, no one was apparently aware of just how stressed Kelly was and how untenable he found his position, so that he killed himself (though there is a conspiracy theory about this too) before the public hearings on his conduct. So protecting people is a priority.

There are other basic principles of journalism too:

- Be curious about the truth
- Ask questions
- Be as transparent as possible about your methods and motives
- Rely on your own original work
- Always check and double check the facts
- Never add anything that is not there
- Do not let spin replace checking facts and sources
- Bring energy to your job
- A lazy journalist gets only half a story, or gets it wrong.

An example of getting a story wrong

Nancy Durham, the VJ interviewed in Chapter 3, is still mortified about an incident that took place some years ago.

She was out filming in Kosovo with a local doctor when war broke out in March 1998. Filming in a hospital she came across a girl soldier who told her a harrowing tale of how her sister had been killed. It featured in the report; her heart-rending account helped make the report a strong one. When Nancy returned to Kosovo she traced the girl and arrived at her house, only to be met at the door by the younger sister who was supposedly dead. When questioned, the girl soldier said she lied because she thought that was what Nancy would want to hear. For Nancy ever since there has been a concern about checking the truth of the story. Difficult to do in a time of war, but still she as a journalist felt she had failed in her job. Luckily there were no repercussions, no one was harmed, and there was no legal redress needed.

Research

The reporting equation is that the greater your preparation and research, the better the end product. Even in breaking news stories, research of the best shots, locations, people to interview and the facts ptoduces a better story. New equals news. Why? Because you have to bring something new to your report, something that will last the day or 24 hours or even longer before it is broadcast. Your research should be able to answer these logistical questions:

- Can it be done?
- Do you have the resources?
- Is there time to do it?
- Is the story accessible?
- Is it affordable?

The possible elements in a report that you might need to research:

- Interview soundbites
- Vox pops (short comments from people usually on the street about the story)
- Pictures relevant to the story
- An opening and a closing or end shot
- Graphics showing statistics or a locating map or a quote
- Extra footage like library shots
- Still shots
- Piece to camera
- Music (though not often in a news piece unless relevant).

Finding facts and figures relevant to the story and background information has become easier with the web. However, you still have to check and double check sources as nothing can be taken for granted just because it is on a website. The best way of corroborating material is by contacting people and a new web source are the blog search engines that allow you to find people. Also telephone directory services globally like teldir.com and infospace.com, and other sites like usenet.com make research possible without leaving your desk. When you interview people for your research (on the phone or face to face) there are checklists. Remember what you are looking to do: to gain the trust of potential interviewees and those who can help further the story.

Remember the example Stuart Ratcliffe from Staffordshire Local TV gave of how he won the trust of the travellers to get their story. He persevered for days by visiting them and just talking, before he got their permission and also an exclusive report.

To do this you have to focus, be organised, informed of basic elements of the story, and have ideas about what your report's elements are. Above all you need a good manner and style of conversation that will get you what you want.

If contact is by e-mail or SMS text then you have to be even more careful in the way you voice your requests so as not to make them appear like demands. The shorthand and casual style of both these modes can quite often cause offence, people taking umbrage at what they see as a lack of politeness, sensitivity and normal courtesies. After all, you need them, they do not necessarily need you.

A basic skill is knowing how to contact people:

- Identify yourself clearly
- Say why you're making contact
- Explain that you need help and of what kind.

During the conversation:

- Ask open ended questions: who, what, when, where, how and why
- Ask simple questions
- *Know* what information you want
- Be polite, interested and above all curious
- Listen to what they say and follow it through
- Don't be aggressive
- Don't make it personal
- Make notes
- Ask for clarification of anything you're unsure of.

Your line of questioning has to elicit the information you need:

- Why is it so important?
- Why is this happening?
- Why do you feel like this, others feel like this?
- Why does this matter?
- Why should people be interested or concerned?
- Why have you done what you have?
- What are you going to do about it?
- What may you do in the future?
- Where can you see what has happened?
- Where can you meet?
- Where might be impacted next?
- Who else is involved?
- Who else might be worth talking to?
- Who do you blame/praise/care about/support/condemn?

At the end of the conversation:

- Check names, title, telephone numbers, e-mails or fax details
- Check *where* the person will be over the next short period of time in case you need to contact them
- Ask if they can suggest anyone else you might talk to
- Thank them and say you might call again.

Of course research is not just about the story – it is also about the visuals, the pictures:

- What is there to see and to film?
- Ask what a place looks like
- Ask if there are any distinctive sounds
- Ask what the mood is
- Ask what people do – thinking of sequences
- Ask for that detail in terms of their routine.

Also think about: if you can't get direct pictures where else can you source them?

- Library footage
- Past events
- Similar location to give as an example
- Online
- Graphics
- Maps
- Animation
- Treated images i.e. stills or moving pictures to use as background
- Stills.

Shots to think about:

- Atmospheric or symbolic/interpretative pictures
- Abstract images of sunsets, feet walking, wheels turning, roads, planes taking off
- General shots of people on streets, buildings
- Aerials or top shots
- People shopping, farming, swimming, doing carpentry, whatever they normally do
- Names of places and companies, identifying pictures
- Opening and closing shots
- Good locations for pieces to camera or live two-ways with the studio, e.g. if you are doing a story about increased traffic on a motorway, a suitable backdrop would be a bridge showing the motorway behind you.

Legal and ethical issues

These are taught at great length on specific courses, but this is a reminder that if you are providing footage especially for news stories, this is what you should bear in mind.

When filming people

Although it can be hard to persuade people to be interviewed, it is surprising how often they agree with no thought of the possible repercussions.

You want to give their names and show their faces on the screen because it strengthens the value of your report; yet you have to be concerned about the consequences of letting their identities become known. The act of naming someone you have interviewed or merely showing their face can be enough to get them into trouble.

Tip: Get the person or people to sign an agreement (you can write it yourself) that the interview or footage can be used. This way you are safe from any legal repercussions.

Example: A common case is that of the 'whistleblower' who has factual or verbal evidence of a company's criminal activities or mismanagement. Do you identify that person, are they prepared to be identified and is the story solid in terms of facts?

Example: A person in an emotional state at a disaster gives an interview which they might not want shown at a later date, when they have recovered or had time to think about it.

So you have to think this through, discuss it with a senior member of a news team or a lawyer, or make the decision yourself, knowingly. In most cases in newsgathering a gatekeeper in the shape of a news editor or producer will check your report before transmission. If you have made a decision first and filmed an interviewee, for example, with their back to the camera then the value of this changes and has to be decided upon merit.

You have to vouch for the fact that the person or people you have interviewed can be shown – in whatever context you are offering it for. No broadcaster or company wants to be sued or to pay out settlement fees.

Legal concerns

These are very particular and every broadcaster has a media lawyer to check anything in a script or the pictures that might result in a legal action, costing the broadcaster a good deal of money. It can be a sackable offence. It can also jeopardise your career.

Most of these pointers are common sense. You do not make a statement that you cannot back up with fact; you use words like *alleged* and *reputed* rather than stating something as a fact; you do not show faces of people if the script makes it seem that it applies to that person.

Example: If the commentary says 'women are increasingly victims of domestic violence', over a shot of a woman looking out of a window, then the viewer could assume this applied to the woman shown. So do not juxtapose the two; change the shot or the words.

Example: The Tanzanian government banned certain skin creams that claimed to whiten skin. Medical evidence pointed to some of these containing ingredients that were potentially carcinogenic. The report talked to: women who had had skin problems as a result of using the creams, a skin cancer specialist, the Ministry of Health spokesperson, an advertising executive about the way they used lighter-coloured models for their campaigns, and an editor of a women's magazine who was promoting 'black is beautiful' in her editorial.

What the report could not do was name those products that allegedly caused problems, nor show them. It had no statement in defence of the products by any manufacturer and the focus of the report was on the ban, but also why men and women wanted to whiten their skin.

A libel case example: Oryx won its libel case against the BBC. The BBC's Ten O'clock News on 31 October 2001 broadcast a Special Report entitled 'The diamonds that pay for Bin Laden's terror'. The report accused Oryx of funding Osama bin Laden and the Al Qaeda network. On 19 November 2001, three weeks later, the BBC broadcast an apology. Oryx Natural Resources sued and was successful in its action against the BBC. The London High Court awarded judgement and costs to Oryx. Geoffrey White, Deputy Managing Director of Oryx, said,

> The BBC never had a shred of evidence for its broadcast. It has now also accepted that it acted irresponsibly. I am delighted that the Court has confirmed this. The broadcast injured Oryx. Our reputation suffered and we sustained enormous financial damage. The BBC will now have to compensate us.

The BBC failed to come up with a convincing defence. Its only claim was that the report was not defamatory. When covering a particular story, if it is likely to offend, upset or provoke a chain of reaction, then you have to consider whether it is worth pursuing. This applies to all kinds of cases which are not in the public view already. Remember Laura McMullan's story in Chapter 3 of wondering whether she should show someone's face:

> I'd never covered a court case and so when I did a piece on a pending court case, I wondered about a picture of the guy accused. The person I asked in the newsroom went crazy and said 'don't use a picture, you can't'. She then offered to write the script for me too! So I'm always checking.

Pitching and proposing a story

Once you've chosen your story, how do you sell it and convince someone that it is worthwhile? Many people find it the most difficult part of journalism because it involves presenting yourself and your confidence in the story or project, as much as selling the actual idea. If you can encapsulate the proposal in one sentence then you stand a good chance of at least having it understood! You would be surprised at how many people never really get to the core of their idea or *why* it matters. Similarly people do not spend enough time researching the programme or website or channel that they are aiming at. If you have not watched a show how can you know what they want or whether your story might fit their brief? Do your homework.

Tips for when you pitch:

- Do not say
  - It's not much of a story but ...
  - I don't *know* whether we could do this but ...
  - I haven't checked it *completely* but ...
  - I *think* I can get the person to speak ...
  - I know it's a long way to go but ...
- Do not
  - Undersell the story
  - Oversell it
- Do
  - Be positive and give an opening sentence that sums it up
  - Explain why it's important/matters
  - Explain how it is possible to film
  - Explain what the logistics are- this would include costs
  - Say what the research shows
  - Be realistic in your pitch
  - Be honest

How to pitch using this format:

- Title (stick to one name for the piece throughout process. Make sure it is easily identifiable)
- Story (sell the story in one or two lines *only*)
- Why are we doing this story now? (one or two lines *only*)
- The peg or realistic date available to air
- Elements (special sequences, access, locations and interviews).

Once successful at getting your proposal accepted, or even if you decide to film something yourself on spec and hope to sell it afterwards, there is a good deal to think about before you set out. Logistics are 90 per cent of filming and only 10 per cent is creativity. If you remember this you cannot fail!

Structuring and writing

Before starting to film it is often best to map out a rough running order and storyline so that you know what you are looking for. This should include questions to ask interviewees too. It is a good discipline and, especially for a

VJ who has to think about the reporting *and* the filming, a reminder of what you need. This is a time-saver, and of incalculable value, as you may well set off immediately travelling or driving to the location and not have any further thinking time. Everything can be refined and changed, but having it roughly in your head is helpful.

Sourcing other material

Graphics

A news report often has extra information in it that is presented in a different format to pictures. Graphics are either a single static page showing key facts or figures or quite literally a graph; or they can be animated. This is a way of highlighting facts especially or even a quote that you as a reporter feel needs to be understood clearly.

Graphics are often 'keyed' or superimposed over an image that is graphically altered in some way to make it paler or changed from negative to positive to make it more interesting. This image can for example be of people at work if the statistics are showing the rise or fall in the number of unemployed.

Graphics are more commonly used in the news studio where a presenter or specialist correspondent stands next to the large screen and talks about a topic, with the graphics coming up as illustration for him or her to point to.

Extra footage

Extra tape or archive film material can be useful for a news report. You can access footage from a tape library within a news organisation, or bought from an outside source like one of the TV news agencies. Film archive material is costly and can take time to order and deliver as it has to be transferred to tape or else a copy made from an existing tape in the archive. However sometimes only archive will do to illustrate a past event. The BBC is now opening its archive to the public and other TV stations will probably follow suit. You can tell when this footage is being used in a news report or a documentary when a caption saying library footage or archive with a date on it is put up on the TV screen.

Other sources of footage include material from amateurs or 'citizen journalists' who have taken unique shots at an event. The rights for this material are negotiated with the individual unless they have sold it on to an organisation. Corporate footage of company headquarters or production processes can be requested from Shell or Microsoft or IBM for example and they often hold what is called B-roll of their activities. If this is used especially illustrating, a past event it also has a caption on it with the date for viewers to understand what is being shown. TV news agencies like APTN and Reuters offer news reports and footage that is used by news channels.

This material is usually paid for by an annual subscription to the service and allows for unlimited access by the large news companies. For an individual it is expensive to buy. Other organisations like charities, NGOs (non-governmental organisations) and the UN hold tape libraries and are often forgotten as possible sources of pictures. Video is so much cheaper to record that even local councils have pictures and regional newspapers have video on their websites and should be remembered as possible sources. There are specialist archives too that are listed in Film Research handbooks, existing worldwide that may have the rare footage you are looking for. As with all research, perseverance can result in you getting something original, unique for inclusion in your report.

Filming

This is the most important part of your work. Without images and soundbites or interviews you have nothing. There is an argument that says photographers are born not made, that some people have an 'eye' for composition and others do not. The same might be said for directing people and 'seeing' how to shoot a sequence, but in truth it can be learnt.

A news report is short, factual and allows for little in the way of super-creative shots. The pictures in a news story are there to illustrate it. Using different lenses like a wide-angle or filters, a lot of camera movement, dramatic lighting or any other effects, sits better with longer reports, mini features, documentary, drama or magazine reports. That is not to say that a wide-angle shot is not useful and sometimes necessary if filming in a tight space, or to give the desired effect, but it is not necessary for a news report. So this reduces the amount of effort you need put into the creative side of filming. However, it does not mean that you can fail to find and film the critical images that tell the story.

Also the filming of those images can and should be done as well as possible in terms of:

- framing a shot, knowing that mid to close up shots work best for impact
- getting the cut-aways (those short usually close-up shots of hands, writing with a pen, eyes, a dog watching, that are used for editing)
- positioning interviewees with a suitable or relevant backdrop, and not against a window, for example, where they cannot be seen
- the same for a piece to camera
- finding a telling opening and closing shot that remind the viewer of the story.

Length of a news report

A standard VJ report that is on BBC World, for example, is two and a half minutes long, around one and a half minutes on national, regional or local news and anything from three to five minutes or even up to 20 minutes on Channel 4 News. (A longer version of seven to twelve minutes is often cut to make more money if you are a freelance and want to sell it to other broadcasters in Europe, the US, Australia etc., or to provide other programmes with different versions for broadcast. For example, a children's or young people's news programme, or a weekly review show could take a long version; news on other channels, for example BBC4, might take a longer piece.) For online and especially newspaper sites, it is interesting to note that one of the main providers of video clips commercially, the Associated Press, offers clips that run from approximately one minute in length, with some as short as 30 seconds or as long as three minutes. Knowing the commission and the eventual placing of the film is helpful, but not critical. What is, is deciding for yourself how much extra material you might shoot in case you want to do a longer version. It all comes down to mathematics.

> Example: A standard news piece is, say, a total of 1 minute 30 seconds.
> Two soundbites between 12–18 seconds in length = 36 secs
> A piece to camera = 12 secs
> Remaining commentary = 42 secs

So you go filming, knowing approximately how much time you have and need to fill.

Filming tips

This section is about tips for filming from VJs, so that you can hear what others do. Every cameraperson develops a personal style of filming. It is inevitable. I prefer extreme close-ups and always getting something strong on the edge of frame, so that like a painting the viewer is drawn in, but everyone is different. There is a basic grammar and also a limitation on the type of shots you can take. However, what changes all the time is your eye and your use of pictures to convey the essence and important points of each story. That is the challenge and also the stimulating part of filming, to capture it, to allow people to see what you see.

Question: What was the hardest part when you first picked up a video camera?

> Remembering to stop waving the camera round and let action leave the frame before repositioning myself.
>
> (Tim Parker)

I was annoyed during interviews that once I was happy I had done everything technically to get the shots right, my journalism would let me down, as my mind would suddenly go blank and I would think 'What should I ask.' Or I would be so absorbed in monitoring the sound that I wouldn't be listening to what the interviewee was actually saying so the result was not as good as it could have been.

(Stuart Ratcliffe)

When I first bought my Hi8 for my new job at BBC World Service TV, I took my wife to a park in Ealing and tried to film her feeding some ducks. It was terrible as I hadn't understood when and how to start and finish a shot. So the stuff was the classic 'tromboning' continually zooming in and out, pans, tilts, every kind of moving shot an editor would find unusable.

(Gareth Jones)

I went to do a piece on child labour at a farm in Lancashire and I remember a videotape editor advising me to 'follow your subjects and don't let them out of your sight', and that's literally what I did. The result was that the camera shots zoomed right, left, everywhere because I was *definitely not* letting the girls out of my sight, or out of shot! Well, I took the tapes back and the piece almost didn't work because there were no cutaways and no one ever left the frame! The editor had to put in a few arty mixes and we just about got away with it.

(Ian O'Reilly)

My first assignment on Hi8 I shot and shot so that I landed up with a shoe box full of tapes and had to turn them into a short feature. It looked so basic, nothing special, no feeling of access because I had gone out and acted like a cameraman and used a tripod all the time. My bureau chief said, 'throw your tripod out the window, go hand-held, go somewhere between breaking and following the rules, to bring something special to your reports.

(Nancy Durham)

Question: What do you try to remember each time you begin filming?

The visual context; what background is best. For sound, how can I best capture it and is the ambient sound a bonus or not.

(Tim Parker)

I found it hard to remember all the things I had to check. White balance, focus, exposure, sound … it seemed if I forgot one then I remembered it next time, but then I would have forgotten something else. I used to have a little checklist in my bag to make sure I had done things.

(Stuart Ratcliffe)

I wrote down notes for reference, troubleshooting notes and a checklist of drills e.g. to make sure the tripod was level and at the right height before you put the camera on it. First decide if you're going auto on everything or not. There's no shame in auto, especially if there's a lot going on around you. I rarely go auto on anything except maybe sound on channel two, that way you know you've always got something usable; on the Z1 it's so good. For focus or exposure I press the auto functions if I'm uncertain to check, but I use the manual functions as much as possible.

(Gareth Jones)

Question: What did you learn the first time that you downloaded your shots and tried to edit them?

I didn't film enough cutaways in length or variation. I learnt that I needed to hold shots longer to be able to edit them.

(Tim Parker)

I was gutted at how little I could use because I wasn't holding the shots long enough.

(Stuart Ratcliffe)

The sound. It was over or under recorded or sometimes on the wrong channel. You have to decide on what sound you want from a situation. So you have to use the right mike and at the right distance for the sound you want and then make sure the levels are right watching the meters in the viewfinder.

(Gareth Jones)

Question: What has got easier the more you film?

The set-ups and directing contributors. I'm getting more confident because even with user-generated and user-authored content it is essential to maintain and link scenes visually. Some shots are the basic grammar so we can't do without them and that makes it easier.

(Tim Parker)

Question: What is your favourite shot?

Pull-focus. A bit cheesy if over-used but always a winner! Don't leave a shoot without one.

(Tim Parker)

I like continuously moving shots which are now my trademark. Rather than going for cutaways during a sequence of action. I try to be as smooth as possible and do it in one shot.

(Stuart Ratcliffe)

The pull-focus shot because it can be poetic and also a wonderful way of saying things in pictures without laying it on with a trowel verbally. I also like filming on the long end of the lens; it can have a lovely effect on the way things look and move.

(Gareth Jones)

Basic camera kit

First, we consider the types of *small lightweight camera* that are available.

For low cost shooting: Sony PD170, PD150, or the VX2000, VX2100E. For high quality shooting: Sony HVR Z1, or the HD version too. For traditional crewing or very high quality production: Sony DSR 500 or 570, or the new DSR-450 which is the replacement for the DSR-570. You now get a flip-out screen and a better head end which should mean better pictures although it still records on tape.

There is also the Panasonic HVX-200; it's the same size as the Sony Z1 but able to record standard definition to tape and HD or SD to P2 card. Also it has adjustable frame rates from 4 to 60 frames per second. The problem is that the single 4 GB card (about 20 minutes of dv) costs £850. Or there is the P2 camera which is a solid state storage medium. Then there are the Canon XLR1 or JVC models too.

Some of the above can also shoot wide-screen, that is 16:9 ratio, which is what most TV is now broadcast in. If not, the cut piece or some rushes, in a news edit suite, have to be ARCed and converted through the Avid edit machine.

Along with your camera, some of which can take different lenses like a wide-angle, is the all-important *tripod*. They come in varying weights and designs. One with a spirit-level on the head is most useful for ensuring that it is straight, before you put the camera on it. Why do you need one? Well, hand-held is fine in a lot of situations, but for filming interviews a lone VJ has to sit or stand next to the camera, also for filming a piece to camera, but apart from logistics, steady shots make it easier on the eye for the viewer and for editing. A tripod also allows you to zoom and to pan or track with the camera, which is difficult hand-held. You have to remember your end objective, to make editing of the shots possible.

The camera has a fixed *microphone*, but the quality is not always good enough for interviews as it records all the surrounding noise too. So a clip or tie mike is invaluable. Light and easy to use, usually with a small battery, it can be plugged into the camera easily. A stick or hand mike can also be part of your kit, as can a small boom mike, that has an extendable handle.

Illustration 6.1 Sony Z1 camera

Illustration 6.2 JVC HD camera

Illustration 6.3 Panasonic HVX 200 tapeless camera

Illustration 6.4 Sony PD150 camera

Radio mikes are also good in allowing greater movement for the interviewee. Everyone has their preferred way of working, but everyone uses an external microphone of some kind to ensure the best sound quality.

Headphones are so important in order to check that you are recording and also for any extraneous sound that might spoil your recording. Without using them you are unable to gauge what is being recorded. Finding out at the edit stage is too late for recovery.

Batteries are needed if, as is usual you are filming away from a mains socket. If you are in a room you can always plug into a socket, saving battery life. Extra batteries are vital to ensure that you can film as much as you want. Extremes of temperature reduce their efficiency and strength. A charger that plugs into your car cigarette lighter, a solar charger or one that in difficult locations can be attached to a car battery or generator is definitely worth having.

Tapes are called mini-dv and are of varying brands and recording lengths. They can be re-used. Tape-less cameras will do away with the need for these.

Lights are not usually part of a standard kit, but there is a camera-mounted light, like a still camera flash, that can be used, and also mini spots that stand on their own tripod legs. Using lights requires extra skill and thinking through. Do stay on manual focus, white balance and keep all the shots for the sequence on the same exposure so that you can edit them together. Otherwise some will be lit and others not. Also if using lights you have to remember the time of day when editing, so to jump from a lit interview to a sunny garden sequence with the same person will appear odd.

There is also the *Camera bag* with *tools* to carry spares in, including tapes, batteries, lenses, lights, screw-driver for the tripod plate when it works loose, a lens cleaning-cloth, spare batteries for the clip mike, and plug adaptors if abroad. A spare small camera is also vital if abroad and investing time and money in a shoot. If one breaks or is stolen, you are unable to proceed.

Tip: Assemble your kit the night before if you are unfamiliar with any of it. Ensure the batteries are charged. Load a new tape in to save time. Use your checklist of equipment to confirm it is all there.

On location allow at least 30 minutes setting up as you will have to choose the interview position and location and also deal with distractions. So arrive early and plan before or request an interview room or space where you can go to set up before the interviewee appears. People are often pressed for time and appreciate you being ready for them. It also gives you time to check your questions and remember your journalistic role.

Health and safety issues are a consideration in whatever company or workplace you find yourself. On the road or out filming there are extra safety issues (even more so if you film abroad). These are basic pointers of potential safety issues. Filming in public places – people tripping over cables or equipment, children and others getting hurt in some way, drawing a crowd, where you are allowed to film e.g. on the pavement, in royal parks, in sensitive areas like airports, theft of equipment if left unattended. Your car –parking, locking, and leaving it unattended in unsafe places. Also driving needs your full attention, so if alone, map reading and long distances need to be worked out carefully. Carrying your equipment – alone you have a tripod plus camera case, plus notebook or even laptop, plus possible extra bag with tapes and batteries. You can easily strain yourself, your back, over-tire and lose track of your gear. You need to remember to take a break and sit down. Communication is important. Keep in touch with base or the relevant person by mobile or other means so that your location is known.

Doing interviews

Reminders: what is the focus of your interview? Do you need the background to show company identification in some form, or to show a geographic location that enhances the story? For example, if the story is about a polluted river, or endangered building then showing it behind the interviewee is helpful. However, it is important that events are not going on directly behind someone that might change and so make editing impossible. Is the person to stand or sit or do something while talking?

Do you need to see their hands because they use them constantly, which means you need a wider shot? The sun has to be in their face not behind them to act as a natural light even if indoors. Placing someone against the light or a window results in a silhouette! Are you going to frame the person

Illustration 6.5 Hand-held filming with a PD150

Illustration 6.6 Filming an interview with a PD150

in a mid-shot or close-up and change the shots during the interview? This is not impossible if you are happy to stop and start the interview. Think about which way you want the person to look – right to left or left to right. Position them always at the side of the frame so it looks more natural that they are looking at someone. If you want to do a reverse shot of yourself asking a question this is important to remember, if they look right to left, then you must look at the camera the opposite way otherwise you cross the 'line'. The line is virtual and all you have to remember is to keep everything as you would see it in real life.

Having someone speak directly into the camera lens is used for effect and if they are telling a story it can work. You have to direct the person as to what you want; otherwise their eye-line can flicker from you to the lens and appear unsettling.

If you are following someone as they are showing you something and talking at the same time you need to be sure you have cutaways and shots to cover what they are doing for editing purposes. Otherwise you will get back and find there is no way you can edit an interview that never changes shot or stops. For example, if someone is showing you what they have discovered at an archaeological site, you need to take separate and 'clean' shots of what is being pointed out, or else, or as well, film the person showing what they are talking about.

Before pressing the record button: check if you are on manual or auto focus, check your sound is working, and check your headphones are on and also working.

Check for any background noise that may prove distracting, like an air conditioner unit that hums, someone banging in the next room, a phone that might ring etc.

Outside sound is also very important to check, as filming always seems to attract road drills, helicopters, microlights and other things which appear out of nowhere. Interviewing at a busy crossroads means you will have bad background noise. You *cannot* separate the sound once back editing it. So choose a quiet location – unless the sound is relevant to the story, but even then you have to be aware of the level.

Once you have hit the record button, you have to position yourself next to the camera and begin your interview. Always watch that the person is talking to you and that their eye-line is constant otherwise they will appear shifty.

Have the courage to stop and start again if there is *any* technical hitch. Also if there is anything you were unhappy with in their reply. You will not get another chance or you will forget to do it. Once you are happy with the replies you have, remember to double check that the tape is fine before you let the person leave.

Doing a piece to camera

If your report needs one or it is requested then a piece to camera or stand-up has to be shot. Where does a piece to camera fit? In the middle of a report as a gear change or to emphasise a point, at the end as a sign-off or at the front if necessary as immediately establishing where you are.

This is by far the most difficult shot to accomplish as a VJ. Another person is very useful, even if you pull in a passerby to stand in for you while you frame the shot. Choose your location carefully in terms of background noise as mentioned above. Obviously you have to use a tripod or if that is impossible you can prop the camera on a wall or get someone else to hold it, but it is less likely to be steady. This does not matter if you are travelling in a boat or car, for example.

Rehearse your words, which you should have written down, and ensure that the length of the piece is appropriate – 10 seconds or 30 words is standard. Record one take and play it back to check on the picture framing and also the sound. Always record more than one acceptable take for safety.

Also, depending on the story, it is always a good idea to record different versions of the words.

Hand-held or not?

The benefit of a small camera is that it is flexible and can convey movement, intimacy and getting into somewhere. So it is used for that effect as a supplementary shot in documentaries, for example, but in news it is used hand-held while travelling, moving around on purpose, in conflicts where there is danger and to give a point of view or perspective. There is a difference between wobbly scope and purposefully planned movement. Many interviews filmed with two or three cameras use the hand-held shot to convey a sense of 'being there' and being 'live' but it can be an annoying and distracting device. For news reports the hand-held shot has to be meant if it is going to show wobbles or shaking. Otherwise a tripod, monopod or steady shot is best – especially for editing. Always remember that walking around continuously filming gives you no 'out' points for editing. You have to have cutaways or additional shots that allow you to edit. Unless you have planned the whole sequence meticulously and direct the person accordingly. Of course hand-held can become your style of filming and become a virtue in your reports, but it does have to be thought through carefully. Just like preparing to paint a picture.

Various shots

A news report is most often neutrally shot with a mixture of establishing or wide shots, some mid and sometimes close-ups (but not extreme) in it. Why is this? The story that the pictures are telling is important and arty or distracting shots are conventionally not used. However, there are a number of shots that can be incorporated and used where relevant and where they help 'make' or tell the story.

- *A tracking shot,* from a moving car, or using laid tracks, or sitting in a wheelchair or supermarket trolley as it is pushed, following a person by walking with them and so on.
- *A pull-focus* from one object in the foreground to another in the background is common for changing emphasis and moving to another person. Or at night on car headlamps.
- *A pan* from right to left or vice versa. If these are too long they can rarely be used in short reports. It has to have a purpose or reason for the pan.
- *A tilt* up or down. For example from a person's eyes to the book they are reading, from a sign outside a building down to the entrance door or vice versa, and so on.
- *A zoom* in or out. For example from a church tower to the whole village, or from a close-up of a tank rolling to see it coming into the wider frame and showing its location.
- *A wide angle* where there is some distortion of the picture which can be used to effect if used with a pan or tilt.
- *A point of view* from over a person's shoulder to show what they are seeing in relation to them.
- *An opening and closing* shot is good for getting the viewer's attention and reaffirming the point of the pictures at the end. Classic shots for ends are sunsets, cars driving away, a door closing and so on. Watch films and see how they end. An opener is usually the best descriptive shot

to show what the story or footage is about. For example, if it is about children in an African village having to walk miles every morning to school, then you would start with a wide shot of them leaving the village or else a close-up of feet walking. If it is storm damage or floods you would try and get the best wide shot to show the extent of the damage before using closer or mid-shots. If it is a tailback on a motorway, again you would need a top shot or wide shot to show it.

Slang terms: pov (point of view), gv (general view), PTC (piece to camera) or stand-up, track (any moving shot), B-roll (background shots).

Filming is something you begin to get a feel for: how to express the visual points you want to make, how best to show something. Everyone has their own style of filming, just as they do in writing or speaking and you should work on developing your 'eye' and visual signature. It is satisfying and creative, but if you just film literally any shots and hope they'll do, you will find it does not pay dividends or work.

An interview with a professional dv camera trainer

Andy Benjamin who trains many BBC staff in what he terms self-op filming has his own views on how to use equipment.

Question: Should you always use a tripod?

My view is you have a vision of what your programme is going to look like so there are no rules on whether or not to use a tripod. It should always come from the story – if you're following ambulance crews at night, you'd have to be hand-held and to set the camera on auto. If you have more time and it is a different sort of film, put it on tripod.

Question: Can someone be taught to have a visual eye?

Some people naturally have better hand/eye coordination than others – it's an aptitude thing. If you look at the way some people move and their style, some are very deliberate and precise, some scatty. In my experience, the latter often have the best programme ideas and are good with people – but not with cameras. So you don't always get both skills. It's like being a bad or good driver.

Question: What is your favourite shot?

I don't personally have one. There's always the thrill of the new in this business and everyone is trying to get a look or new style. Some tend to overuse shots. In drama at one stage it was the NYPD Blues [American police series] style of shooting – never cut but with whip pans. This was all rehearsed moves and is difficult to copy. Then there's Louis Theroux style because it is all about his view of things and presenter-led. So the camera shots are from his perspective and from behind him, also filmed in one continuous shot. The programme producer felt if you cut a lot, the viewer thought they were missing things. Once you've got that sort of real time sequence you can use it whole. Pull-focus is difficult to do on the small cameras because of the chip size. I don't recommend it. But for a deep two-shot then alright, it is an interesting device but if used in the wrong way, a little focus-pull looks like a mistake not an effect.

After filming

After filming the process goes on. The shots have to be viewed and logged or in any case noted; the commentary or script written and recorded. A good format is to use a table in MS Word and to write a rough running order for your story, with possible shots against the words (see Table 6.1).

Before you write your script:

- Make a plan, writing notes and bullet points before you write
- Put down interviews and quotes
- Facts and figures
- Look again at your rough running order. Use this as the basis for your script
- The script, storyline or narrative is the key to a report
- A script is determined by maths: three words per second
- Research defines the content
- The role of images
- Soundbites have to be short, 15–20 seconds
- Remember what your piece to camera says
- Lay out your script as in Table 6.1.

Table 6.1 Running order and possible shots

Commentary	Pictures
This is the morning after the worst floods the West Country has ever seen	Wide shot of flooded streets
People are still being rescued from the roofs of their houses by boats and helicopters	Person being helped to safety
PTC 'Behind me is the main town square with all the cars submerged'	Reporter in vision with flooded square behind

Writing

- Open with a short sentence. Why? It focuses the reader on the story and you the writer on the telling
- The first sentence should encapsulate, titillate and make the viewer want to keep watching
- Think about giving details: time, place, date, ages, quantities
- Set the scene so the viewer can be there with you: just one phrase or sentence can do it
- First sentence to be followed by a second that details why you should stay interested, starting to unravel or tell the story
- Keep up the pace: whether a feature or news piece, the story-telling has to develop
- Use an active verb and not a passive one. That means 'The train crashed into the car stalled on the tracks' rather than 'The car stalled on the tracks was crashed into by the train'.

Make the writing interesting

Example: 'A multiple car crash in Birmingham's city centre has this morning claimed the lives of 16 people'. Rather: '16 people were killed this morning in a multiple car crash in Birmingham city centre'.

Try not to use slang, jargon or clichés. Examples: sparked off, sixty-four-dollar question, infrastructure, nitty-gritty, brass tacks, in the red, took a dive, top of the table, wheeler-dealer, grass-roots, spin doctors, only time will tell, the future looks bright, no end in sight, beginning of the end, by and large.

Avoid over-used or abused metaphors. Examples: targets being exceeded, bottlenecks being cured, bridges crossed.

Cut your calories: use words that count. Hit the delete key and lose your adjectives. They are imprecise. A 'massive' earthquake happens one week and then another one a week later; what does 'massive' mean? A 'big' fire – whose scale of reference?

All of the above are often used and are part of what is known as 'journalese'. Watch any news bulletin and see how many you can identify.

Once you've written the script, consider this checklist:

- Is the top-line of the story sufficiently supported?
- Has someone double-checked, called or visited all the phone numbers, addresses or web addresses in the story? What about names and titles?
- Is the background material required to understand the story complete?
- Are all those in the story identified and have they been contacted and given a chance to talk if required?
- Does the story take sides or make value judgements?
- Is anything missing?
- Are all the quotes accurate and properly attributed and do they capture what the person really meant?

Logging

Logging takes time and yet it helps you to identify time codes for your material, to look again at what you have shot, which shots are usable and where the soundbites are and how long they are. Playing back your material can either be done on your camera or when you download your material onto your pc, through your edit software programme.

A log can use the same table format as the running order and script. You can just add the time codes to your script as well (see Table 6.2 and 6.3). If like the local TV VJs in Chapter 4, you are working against the clock, a much rougher logging or jotting down of the shots you want can be done, or if you are so sure of your story and have shot a small amount of footage then you can grab the shots as you download and then assemble your edit as you go.

Editing on a PC or laptop

Software programmes for editing to a professional standard are usually Avid or Adobe Premier Pro or if using a Mac, Final Cut Pro. Every PC today comes with an editing package which is useful for doing your own personal editing and for practising with. The programmes have to be learnt, but are not difficult to work with. In fact they allow you to edit creatively with an array of effects that can keep you occupied for hours experimenting. A news report or straightforward cutting of sound and pictures does not

Table 6.2 Logging shots

Time code showing hours, minutes and seconds	Commentary	Pictures
00.03.22– 05.30 Choice of shots in these 2 minutes	This is the morning after the worst floods the West Country has ever seen	Wide shot of flooded streets
00.06.30–07.50 Either one shot or several in these times	People are still being rescued from the roofs of their houses by boats and helicopters	Person being helped to safety
11.40–55 i.e. 15 seconds	PTC: Behind me is the main town square with all the cars submerged ...	Reporter in vision with flooded square behind

Table 6.3 A brief log of shots

Time code		Shot
Tape 1	00.00.00–04.50	GVS of floods
	1.35	Close-up of swimming dog
	3.28–35	Water pouring shot

usually require more than cuts between shots, but fades or dissolves can be used depending on the programme and eventual output source and taste of the news editor or producer who is taking your material. Also each story demands certain effects and for a softer human interest story, for example, dissolving from one scene to another may be acceptable, but not for a story about a foreign conflict or a hard-edged political story. In order of importance, editing has to:

- Ensure the report or story is understandable
- Be to time or an accepted length
- Have good sound levels
- Maintain a pace and interest
- Include a commentary track
- Include captions if that is the house style (or else caption details to be sent together with the script)
- Include other source material including library footage, any still photos or shots of relevant documents etc. that are needed for the story, graphics which have relevant statistics, facts or figures, written quotes.

It is easy to do graphics and captions for interviewees as well as for information.

A house style, e.g. the font used and coloured strap, is important plus a logo of the programme. Often the name straps, captions or Astons are put on live during studio transmission, but each programme, bulletin and channel has its own way of doing things.

Recording commentary

This can be done before editing and used as a track to cut the pictures too, or else pictures and soundbites can be assembled first and then a voice track or commentary added to link the story elements. Each person has their preferred way of doing it. If time is a pressure then writing and recording the commentary first is the fastest way. The commentary can be recorded straight onto your pc, but the noise around may make going into a quieter space and recording into your camera the better option. This is then downloaded off your tape as with the shot footage. Again depending on the gatekeepers and who has to check the script, it may be that the commentary is only a guide and then is finalised at the last moment, or else that it is changed in some ways, or passed.

For freelance VJs sending in a cut report, a script is often sent in with a guide commentary or a separate commentary track is recorded, to allow for editing or for re-voicing by someone else. For VJs just sending in footage that has been bought to be cut or put into another report, a log of the shots and the people interviewed is important.

Captions

The names of interviewees have to be checked and double-checked for spelling and their title. Also captions for the dates of archive footage have to be accurate.

Tips: The best way to learn and improve your own editing style is to watch output and see how people approach cutting, the effects they use, and whether they work for you as a viewer or not. Also to watch feature films, documentaries and other genres like pop promos, videos or advertisements to see how they are edited. Remember that if your material is going out online then the size of the screen is much smaller, and the definition much less, so that the shots you choose need to be able to take a drop in quality for play-out.

Summary

Recording video needs preparation, consideration and organisation.

Once you have mapped out a plan of action, filming should be enjoyable, creative and rewarding. Compare it to cooking a meal for some friends. Do you just hope the meal will come together in some way, or do you plan it, read some recipes or ask for advice, write down the ingredients you need, go out and buy them and then come back to cook? Just picking up a camera, switching it on and 'having a go' is fine but not if your objective is to be professional and to use it for work. Even for personal use and say uploading onto your own blog site or for friends and family to watch, I would argue that the more planning that goes into it, the better the quality of the footage and the better the response.

Questions for students

1   How do you identify a story?
2   How do you pitch a story?
3   Is writing a rough script before you go out filming useful?
4   What are the rules to remember when writing a script or commentary?
5   Are there legal concerns to do with filming, and if so what are they?

7 Videojournalism and new media

Broadband access to the internet with its high-speed connection and interactivity is the basis for what is called 'new' media. No one could have predicted how the 'information super highway' that former US Vice-President Al Gore described as a future possibility was going to change our lives, bring about a cultural revolution and help initiate a new meritocracy. In a short space of time, a large part of the world has crossed personal, local, national and international frontiers in communication. If this sounds excessive, just think of what you do online and of how much you can do. The odds are that you are no longer a passive viewer of linear TV but that you actively use the internet outside your work hours, have favourite websites you have signed up to and that you maybe blog, or upload pictures or video using your video camera, mobile phone, digital camera and pc. If this is the case then you are using 'new' media tools.

New media is the means by which a wide range of communication is carried out via the internet: news, PR, business, entertainment, sports, education, information and personal interaction. So it is watching TV, films or events live on your computer, or downloading for later viewing using an iPlayer or media player or its equivalent; or maybe uploading your own material onto YouTube or MySpace to share with others. Using RSS feeds to send and receive written and audio-visual material is one of the growth areas for both work and pleasure and these can be received on your mobile, via e-mail or to your personal digital organiser (PDA), like a Blackberry. Networks like Skype allow for interactive and video phone calls via broadband doing away with the need for mobiles – a technology now used for newsgathering when a small webcam is attached to a pc. The list of possibilities is always being updated and there is no end in sight.

New media offers information and communication on demand when you want it. Your location, time and the reason for a search or action is not relevant to the successful accessing or sending of material – it can be done day or night. Interactive networking for social and business requirements is now standard; can you remember what life was like without a mobile phone, or without e-mails? The speed at which people globally are incorporating each new technology into their communication skills is unparalleled. For example, blogging was on the fringes for some years before it was taken up by people in sufficient numbers for it to become a force and now to enter the mainstream, existing alongside and merging with journalism, the corporate and advertising worlds. Video blogs, or vlogs, are multiplying too.

So which out of all these new media tools are relevant to you as a student, as a potential videojournalist or looking for a career in the media? Well, understanding what the new media tools are and how you might use them in your career or even personal life is a good starting point.

In this chapter we will look in depth at what has now been established: internet broadcasting and video communication, including blogging, podcasting, video-streaming, the role of RSS feeds and mobcasting via phones. Understanding where all this is leading, how the future might look in this field, will be covered in the next chapter, where convergence is the theme. In his role as postmodernist and videojournalism crystal ball gazer, the American Terry Heaton predicted with remarkable accuracy the changes that would benefit not just VJs but anyone interested in new media and media delivery via new technology. His belief that universities will respond to new media is prescient.

> Universities will begin to abandon the idea of broadcast journalism as a degree option and steer young people to the multimedia skill set required for local journalists of the future. While many universities have begun teaching multimedia journalism, the broadcast journalism degree remains (probably because people will still pay for it). This will change, as counsellors begin moving people to multimedia and videojournalism degrees rather than broadcasting. The media industry will demand it.

Why the media and communications industry will demand it, is because everything is affected by new and multimedia technology and no company can afford to ignore it. Remember that the key change is in everybody needing a web presence; a site is now a must-have and as a portal it has to be interactive and multi-media. It is no longer enough to have a front page with nothing on it for visitors to access. Expectations are now for getting information in numerous ways and these have to be presented on site and online. Online banking, shopping, paying bills, booking travel and buying tickets are personal activities, but for work too, finding key facts and figures, locations and latest press releases and company information is all via the internet. To work in public relations, advertising or marketing, as part of an online team, or in the communications departments of the civil service, any commercial business or even charity, all of whom have new media needs, an understanding of what the tools are is key. Most of these incorporate video, re-emphasising the need for VJ skills. Certainly TV and shortly print newsrooms expect interns and new graduates to have a working knowledge of web skills and of video filming and possibly editing, over and above the normal journalism skills. So we are going to look at these different sectors in turn: internet broadcasting, blogging, video blogging or vodcasts, podcasts, RSS feeds and SMS messaging, plus mobcasting and citizen journalism.

Broadcasting

The moving of audiences away from watching conventional linear TV channels to viewing via broadband on their pcs is now well-documented and widely reported. The trend is to watch your favourite programmes that you have downloaded onto a PVR (personal video recorder) in your own time, or watching instead alternative and independent internet channels. These are launching in the US and the UK to capture the growing market of people who now search for and choose new sources for their news, information and entertainment needs. More importantly people *contribute* to websites and aggregators by sending audio or user-generated videos or just posting comments, and so feel part of them in a unique way. MySpace.com, YouTube, Bebo, GoogleVideo, Heavy.com, Trouble, Current TV, or Microsoft's MSN are websites and 'channels' that are household names. Their heavy traffic, YouTube has 100 million video clips viewed every day, has attracted the big media players who see falling conventional TV viewing figures and are trying to capture the new-style audiences. Even more exciting is that the market is open to small players with a good idea. For example, Dailymotion, a French site popular in Spain too, launched last year, at about the same time as YouTube. Dailymotion has not come close to its American rival, but Benjamin Bejbaum, the young co-founder, now boasts one billion page hits in February 2007 alone. He has attracted $320,000 (or about £160,000) in venture capital money and is trying different ways to sell advertising. He has yet to be bought out, but M&A (mergers and acquisition) fever has hit the broadband sector. MySpace has been bought by Rupert Murdoch (as already mentioned) and he also has linked in now to YouTube. YouTube was a garage start-up in classic Silicon Valley style in 2005. The original idea was to give people a place to post or upload any clip of video of less than ten minutes so long as it was not pornographic and copyright free. For this service you sign up and use the easy technology. Similarly as a viewer it is quick to run videos and to search. The aim too was to store every music video ever made on the site and a link-up with Warner Music lets the company place its artists' videos on it, as well as allowing the footage to be used by YouTube filmmakers too. Now with Google buying YouTube for $1.65 billion (around £850 million) in 2006 and BSkyB linking with Google to 'deploy its suite of search, advertising, communications and video services', the sites are linking-up. In other words, BSkyB will launch a user-generated video service that will run off Google's video content tools, offer a version of G-mail and share advertising revenue with Google. At the same time YouTube has linked with US mobile firm Verizon Wireless to allow subscribers to Verizon's Vcast services to view content on the YouTube website via their mobiles and also to post clips from their phones via a wireless network as opposed to via e-mail. This will doubtless spread to the UK where already UK mobile operators are trying to expand their services, with O2 offering LookAtMe where clips can be posted and downloaded, and '3' mobile network provider with its Kink Kommunity. Sony Pictures Entertainment recently paid $65 million (or around £33 million) for Grouper, an internet company that specialises in user-generated video, another sign that many of the established media companies feel they cannot do without a new media acquisition.

British Telecom, the UK's largest tele-communications provider, in December 2006, jumped on the bandwagon and launched its BTVision offering a broadband TV service. Its deal with Irish sports broadcaster Setanta will allow it to show live Premiership football games. Vodafone UK will be the exclusive mobile network partner offering BT. Future communications will allow you to chat using video telephony (like Skype) and offer a platform for user-generated content so you can share videos, photographs and music with a wider audience. Features mean TV content can be watched when you want and is not tied to TV schedules. There is no regular monthly subscription. There is also access to a library of on-demand content via broadband, plus 40 Freeview channels. All this comes via a new set-top box, the V-box, which is a personal video recorder (PVR) able to store up to 80 hours of content, pause or rewind live TV and record programmes at the touch of a button. The box is also HD-ready. Ian Livingston, BT Retail chief executive repeated what is now the new media mantra:

> it is all about giving control to the viewer – control over what they watch, when they watch it and how they pay for it. We believe that broadband can transform television and take it into a new era.

Flextech is another company also hoping to link their TV channels, especially Homegrown to online via their Trouble.com site that is aimed at the 16–24-year-old market. It is a copy of YouTube allowing visitors to upload video clips by computer or phone and to watch content. ITV in January 2007 relaunched their broadband service that from March 2007, via a media player, allows viewers to watch TV shows up to 30 days after broadcast and also to watch simulcast TV broadcasts for free. Access to the ITV archives is also being offered, a feature seen as desirable and following the BBC's lead to open their archives for access.

One of the highest profile new internet channels as opposed to portals is Current TV. It is the brainchild and co-owned by former US Vice-President Al Gore, whose move into media has been highlighted following the release of his documentary *An Inconvenient Truth* about the dangers of global warming. Following in the footsteps of Michael Moore it has done big box-office business and helped his online channel. Launched in the summer of 2005, Current TV is a 24 hour TV channel that runs as a democratic venture. It allows users to vote on the quality of video clips, creating what is a meritocracy, far removed from the old media style of designated people deciding what is news and newsworthy. (Think back to Chapter 5 where we discussed how a news team led by a news editor decides on what is news, and how different this venture is.) You pay to upload your videos, and no doubt if a video got enough attention like a blog it could be bought by a network, but that is not the intention – it is to create an alternative to mainstream news. The viewers vote, create programmes and can put their own reports and films on the channel. Viewer-created content accounts for 30 per cent of the channel's airtime and is rising. It reportedly reaches more than 30 million homes in the US and a venture with Sky (another Murdoch link-up) will see it from spring 2007 in the UK. Sky believes it will reach one in three UK homes. 'Current TV harnesses the energy and excitement of the internet to enable viewers to create their own content', Gore says. 'It is the first TV network created by, for and with a young audience largely aged 16 to 34'. Gore and his business partner Joel Hyatt have managed to tap into the high internet users. The channel has extensive online tutorials, tips and hints from famous film and TV personalities on how to produce video reports, on storytelling and camera technique, and what equipment to use. Regular contributors are paid. So it attracts aspirant videographers and VJs who can contribute three to eight minute videos on a number of topics. The US version of Current TV has even got site visitors making adverts for the sponsors. These include L'Oréal, Gap, Levi, Sony-Ericsson and Toyota. 'We're creating a powerful new brand of television that does not treat audiences as mere viewers, but as collaborators', Gore says. The news bulletins on the channel are very different from traditional reports. In collaboration with Google the reports played out are those that got the highest number of hits during the day. The channel is yet to make a profit, but it is, market watchers say, early days.

Britain's first political internet TV channel launched in 2006, called 18DoughtyStreet Talk TV. It is to broadcast four hours a night Monday to Thursday from studios in central London with a mix of pre-recorded and live programmes. Its purported aim is to provide opinionated and controversial reports and programming, to break what they term the balanced and objective reporting on established current affairs programmes. The main presenters in the studio are two well-known bloggers, both with conservative leanings.

The channel hopes to have a core website with blogs where comments can help shape the programmes, as will the daily votes on which news story will make it into the headlines. It wants to give out dv cameras to establish a network of 100 citizen journalists/reporters nationwide who can film reports. A press release said,

> We believe that within the next twelve months people will start watching internet TV through their normal TV screens. Few people realise that every TV screen has a plug in the back to which a computer can be connected.

The channel will use the latest streaming technology to broadcast live and all programmes will be available for later download. Programmes are also pod or vod-castable. The format for Current TV, for 18DS, and for the well-presented US site hotair.com is becoming a standard one. The key factor is that all these channels rely on the general public for unpaid contributions and to make the site work. The question is just how much energy and enthusiasm the general public has for spending time producing videos and contributing their views and news. In America a wave of indignation over the Iraq war and the perception that the established media connived with the government has fired up the blogging community and those alternative internet sites where opinions can be heard. Whether or not the same strength of opinion exists to keep these sites afloat in the UK and Europe, let alone the rest of the world, remains to be seen.

What is more sure is that small start-ups offering services are beginning to proliferate, like TIOTI.com, standing for 'tape it off the internet', who source where and when you can download shows online including from Apple's iTunes and Amazon's download services. Started by a Blackpool graphic designer Paul Cleghorn, the site is filling those gaps in online entertainment services. No doubt before this book is in the bookshops, a number of other sites will have been launched and also internet channels, offering not only news but all kinds of participatory programming. The key change then is that the internet together with broadband can offer those visionaries and entrepreneurs a medium that allows for new styles of two-way communication.

Traditional TV channels have had to keep up with new media developments that are now an acceptable part of our Web culture. As the BBC has described it, offering content for people 'on the go' and 'on demand'. For the BBC one important wake-up call came after an analysis of how people viewed the Eurovision Song Contest in 2006. It was on TV, but the BBC offered a digital interactive service and the chance to download videos from each of the 39 participating countries via its Broadband Player and WAP portal. Eleven per cent of the Eurovision audience requested video streams on the Web and through their mobile phones. This was the signal that people wanted it delivered their way. An unbundling of news and programming has happened so fast that you are not aware of how recently it was that you first heard a sign-off, for example by the regional Meridian news programme presenter, saying, ' That's all from us now but for those of you who want to keep up to date there is our internet channel www.itvlocal.tv. We're back with our next bulletin at ...'.

BBC TV's website is now one of the most visited sites worldwide and they pride themselves of staying ahead of the new media game. All TV channels have also begun to update their newsgathering techniques using web-based technology, besides offering a full range of web-based watching and listening services. The following example shows how regional journalists used technology to best effect. BBC TV South scooped their rivals Meridian by an entire day, using a broadband connection, a small dv camera and a laptop – a sign of things to come.

The occasion was the 21st anniversary Virgin Atlantic flight from Heathrow to New York where journalists Paul Clifton and Alex Dunlop were on board, along with other press teams. The plane landed at 6 pm UK time; by 6.35 their video had arrived as an email file in Southampton; and at 6.47 the report was on air – the last item on the regional bulletin. How did they do it?

'We knew time was tight', Clifton said, 'so we boarded the flight with a PD150camera, a laptop and a lip mike [a microphone that you can hold close to your mouth for better sound quality]'. They then interviewed Richard Branson on board, and downloaded it into the laptop, where they had already loaded graphics and archive material. They then wrote and recorded the script and edited the piece before landing. On arrival at JFK airport they shot Branson next to the plane and a piece to camera. Then, Clifton said,

> We ran to the nearest wireless broadband point in the airport. It took ten minutes to finish adding the new shots, another six minutes to compress the file and a further twelve minutes to send the file wirelessly to a computer in Southampton.

The BBC South Today producer Liesl Smith said the turnaround had 'opened up a whole new world of opportunities. It was a triumph for small cameras, mobile editing and mobile transmission via the internet'. It was also done by journalists or VJs practised in the whole range of new media techniques. The allure of these methods too is that they are far cheaper than the investments that are made in purchasing conventional professional-standard newsgathering equipment.

Mobile phone usage

TV news stations and channels are also delivering content to mobile phones – and entrepreneurs have been quick to provide specially filmed and produced mobile content. Sky News says it has tens of thousands of subscribers to its news streaming. The small size of the mobile screens limits the length of clips that can be sent and also the time that a user might want to watch. However, the larger hand-helds or PDAs, already being used in Japan, allow for better viewing and are a sign again of the future still to come. Mobile-videocasting as a video technique is part of what has been called the 'citizen journalist' or 'user-generated content' revolution. There is some confusion as to the use of the term mobcasting that began applying both to footage being shot on mobiles and also podcasts to mobiles. So I have used the term mobile-videocasting to distinguish it from the sending of audio files. It is now widely called UGC or user-generated content to distinguish it from professional material and has the potential of being developed into an alternative and acceptable newsgathering technique as the mobile cameras improve in quality, not to supplant other newsgathering techniques but as another tool for videojournalism and VJs – and also citizen journalists.

The influential US magazine *Time* decided in December 2006 to name its Person of the Year, not an individual, as it traditionally does, but as 'you' – or us, individual users. User-generated content represents a 'story about community and collaboration on a scale never seen before', the publication wrote in an editorial. So UGC has officially joined the ranks of new media. UGC has, on the back of a number of world disasters and events, become an accepted medium. The hanging of Iraq's former leader Saddam Hussein on 30 December 2006 was captured on a mobile phone and posted on the internet for the world to see. There was the mobile footage of the tsunami wave filmed by citizen reporters and without their visual testimony no one, who was not there, would have known what it was like or what the waves looked like. The events of 7 July 2005 in London, when people travelling to work were caught up in the bombs that went off, were filmed by those on the spot using their mobiles. They were trapped in the Underground and their journeys stopped by events. The broadcasters, namely Sky News, ITV News and BBC News, asked viewers to send in their footage. The result was that they were inundated. Ben Rayner, the editor of the ITV News channel, says ITN was sent more than a dozen video clips from mobile phones – some so graphic as to be unusable – and they played an important role in getting across to viewers the nature of the story. 'It's the way forward for instant newsgathering, especially when it involves an attack on the public', he believes. Videos shot in smoke-filled London Underground tube trains of people stumbling in the semi-darkness, of the No. 30 bus shattered by a bomb and horrific scenes of body-strewn roads were among the most powerful images to be sent in. John Ryley, the executive editor of Sky News, says,. 'It raises questions for the authorities but these devices allow a democratisation of news. News crews usually get there just after the event, but these pictures show us the event as it happens'. It is now seen as a turning point in broadcasting history. All the bulletins ran mobile phone sequences shot by members of the public for the first time. Another example in the UK was in July 2006 when a giant inflatable sculpture on display in a park in Co. Durham blew free from its moorings. A number of people were inside the inflatable at the time and two were killed. The accident was filmed by spectators on their mobile phones and immediately sent in to the TV networks, which ran the pictures on the news that day. The police appealed for any footage to be sent in to them too to help in their inquiries into the tragedy. So the footage is performing a civic role as well and while the police have yet to use mobiles for crime reporting they already use small video cameras in their work. The phenomenon of UGC has gone hand in hand with new media developments on the web. Also mobile-videocasting can be developed for artistic and creative videos, using albeit cruder and shorter clips for drama sequences, say, but as the technology develops this too can expand its use. Where the small dv cameras first revolutionised the news market with their grainy and hand-held shots, the mobile phone cameras are doubtless going to follow with a new style of video filming.

Blogging

Blogging has now developed from being a simple personal weblog, an observational diary written online, into a layered new media tool where video blogs, or vlogs, audio blogs or podcasts can be posted and sent from mobile phones to blog sites and vice versa. You can make easy links from your blog directly to the flickr.com website too, where your photos can be seen.

Blogs, like books and newspapers, come in every conceivable shape, type and quality. The definition by the first server for blog writing, Blogger. com is:

> A blog is a personal diary. A daily pulpit. A collaborative space. A political soapbox. A breaking-news outlet. A collection of links. Your own private thoughts. Memos to the world.

Where do they exist? In the blogosphere, a virtual space online. Why or how, you might ask, did anyone conceive of this idea? Well, the technology changed and so in 1997 an American, David Winer, who believes he was the first, decided to have a go at writing onto what was before inaccessible websites. It was the same as before CDs became writable and recordable: you could read or watch one but not change it. Winer was followed by other now luminaries like Robert Wisdom, Tomalak's Realm and Camworld. It was not until 2003 that blogging took off as the software to write them became user-friendly. It now takes three steps on any of the blog servers like blogspot. com to sign up and start writing. Today a blog is created almost every second and there are millions of them out there, not all active but the blogosphere has within the space of a few years become a force to be reckoned with. It has challenged conventional journalism, the establishment and government in a number of countries and led the way for interactivity online in all its latest forms.

One debate has been about the status of bloggers versus journalists, as the success of bloggers in force has rudely awakened those journalists who felt they might be usurping them. In fact bloggers are not on the whole trying to unseat journalists, but they have challenged many who have stopped researching and trying for primary sources for stories. It is most likely that blogging will continue to exist as an alternative form of conveying information, comment and opinion of all sorts to anyone out there who wants to listen. Their power? Well they brought down Dan Rather – the revered presenter of the US network CBS' *60 Minutes* programme. They did this by proving that he was wrong in quoting Bush's service record. Bloggers buzzed so long and hard about this and displayed the documents reconstructed to show they were fake, that the White House was forced to release the relevant memos which showed that Rather was wrong. He had to apologise and was forced to resign.

> We see you behind the curtain … and we're not impressed by either your bluster or your insults. You aren't higher beings, and everybody out here has the right – and ability – to fact-check … and call you on it when you screw up and/or say something stupid. You, and Eason Jordan, and Dan Rather, and anybody else in print or on television, don't get free passes because you call yourself 'journalists'.
>
> (Vodkapundit blogger Will Collier responding to CJR Daily Managing Editor Steve Lovelady's characterisation of bloggers as 'salivating morons')

Could bloggers be called the fifth estate, after journalism as the fourth? Thomas Carlyle called them that, but attributed the phrase to Edmund Burke. (The other three estates are priesthood, aristocracy and commoners.) Either way Carlyle wrote that is you 'invent writing, democracy is inevitable. … Whoever can speak, speaking now to the whole nation, becomes a power, a branch of government, with inalienable weight in law-making, in all acts of authority'. Well, a survey of political blogs by Pew Internet and American Life Project in May 2005, a market research company focussed entirely on the internet, revealed that they sometimes lead and sometimes follow the mainstream media. And they are not always successful. For example, during the Bush election campaign he was thought during the live debates to have had a suspicious bulge in the pocket of his jacket. Bloggers queried this, asking whether it was a microphone. But it was not picked up and he was not forced to explain himself.

There are now famous super-bloggers like the Blogger of Baghdad, Salam Pax. In the run-up to the war, Pax wrote a compelling journal of daily life in the Iraqi capital, posted regularly on his weblog. While many readers celebrated his insider's view of the impending war, others wondered about his authenticity. He has gone on to do network TV reports, proving that blogging can be a breeding ground for talent.

In the US Andrew Sullivan, Jeff Jarvis of Buzzmachine and Jay Rosen of PressThink are helping set the news agenda because newspapers refer to their posts (or writings) on their blog-sites. They focus on the new media – how they're evolving, what's broken, why cultural and technological changes matter. These people are the warriors 'who put on their armour and sit down at the typewriter to do battle, and judge their success by how many dragons they slay that day', says David D. Perlmutter, a senior fellow at Louisiana State University's Reilly Centre for Media and Public Affairs. Interestingly, for all the US journalists' dismissal of bloggers, some 41 per cent of journalists access blogs at least once a week and 55 per cent say they read blogs as part of their work duties, according to a 2005 University of

Connecticut study. Bloggers appear to be influencing mass communication in three ways, according to Pew's May 2005 report, 'Buzz, Blogs and Beyond' (http://www.pewinternet.org/PPF/r/43/presentation_display.asp) by policing the media, first, with the example of Dan Rather's demise. Second, by providing a sounding for 'journalists, activists, and political decision-makers [who] have learned to consult political blogs as a guide to what is going on in the rest of the Internet'. Third, bloggers are becoming pundits in their own right, like Salam Pax, and in the US, many of them are being interviewed on various media platforms: cable, TV and radio; or presenting programmes like those on the UK political internet channel 18 Doughty Street.

The mainstream media has done what every established sector does when under threat and that is to assimilate the new with the old. So, newspapers are running journalists' blogs on their websites and sometimes publishing them on their print pages too. These are not always interactive as on the main blog servers, but they are personalised accounts and diaries giving often interesting behind the scenes glimpses of newsgathering and also of personal perceptions. Maintaining blogs is time-consuming but a necessary evil according to newspaper and TV editors alike. Inevitably the blogosphere is being hijacked by companies and advertisers who see it as the tool for electronic public relations. Personal comments mean that for journalists using blogs for research, they have to tread carefully on the minefield of what may or may not be true. As in the advice on producing reports in Chapter 6, VJs and journalists have to check and double check their facts and sources.

> It will take a tough hide, a tougher one than journalists maybe are used to, as they sort out their new relationship with a more interactive audience. But journalism has no value, nor any claim to authority, except in the name of citizens … I think many news organisations have already found it remarkable how much the tone of an angry audience member can change if you simply listen attentively and respond fairly.
>
> (Tom Rosenstiel, director of the Project for Excellence in Journalism)

That is the name of the game, interactivity. Blogging is seen by some as the second internet revolution. It has also caused considerable concern for companies concerned about employees writing blogs in their work time but also about the blog content. Of course it is fine if you are writing a requested corporate blog, but even then checking a chief executive has not given away information inadvertently has to be done. The very casual or more relaxed tone and nature of a blog has its dangers. As a result guidelines have been drawn up by a number of companies. Restrictions are placed on talking about anything of a confidential nature in their workplace, and on damaging the reputation of a company, brand or employee. For example, an employee in Waterstones Bookshop in Edinburgh consistently talked in his blogs about where he worked – easy enough to identify it without naming the store. He was extremely rude about his boss. The result – he was fired. As was the air hostess who posted photos of herself in semi-pornographic poses wearing her uniform.

A blogging glossary has emerged with many words now part of our everyday vocabulary as the technology becomes more familiar to us.

Blogging glossary

- Aggregator
  A piece of software used by webloggers and others who want to check a large number of news sources or weblogs on a daily basis. Aggregators regularly check selected RSS feeds (see RSS) for new content and display a list of results, usually listing the most recently updated links first, allowing bloggers to quickly catch up on the latest news and comment from around the web.
- Blawg
  A weblog that deals with legal issues, often written by lawyers or academics.
- Bleg
  To use one's blog to beg for assistance (usually for information, occasionally for money). One who does so is a 'blegger'. Usually intended as humorous.
- Blogdex
  A project from MIT's Media Lab that regularly checks what weblogs are linking to, thus tracking information as it flows across the blogosphere. By going to the Blogdex you can see which links are most popular on weblogs at the moment. A high ranking on Blogdex is both an indicator that your weblog is getting lots of traffic, and also a guarantee that your weblog will get lots of traffic, as readers click through from the Blogdex index.
- Blogger
  Blogger is both the truncated name for a weblogger, and the name of one of the oldest weblog publishing services Blogger, the web service. It is now owned by Google.
- Bloggerati
  Big name bloggers who, by dint of their weblog's longevity and/or quality, and their propensity to champion and comment on the weblog phenomenon, have become well-known among other bloggers. Derived from 'literati'.
- Blogistan
  The totality of blogs; blogs as a community.
- Blogorrhea
  An unusually high volume output of articles on a blog.

- Blogosphere
  The world of weblogs or the community of bloggers, as in 'the blogo-sphere is alive with the news of Saddam Hussein's capture'. Some bloggers also refer to the blogging community as 'Blogistan'.
- Blogroll
  A list of links to other blogs, often included in a vertical column down one side of the weblog: usually a way of illustrating the blogs you read or value.
- Comments
  A facility that allows weblog visitors to leave their comments on the author's views. Some high-profile webloggers have been forced to remove the comment facility because of abusive or legally risky contributions from readers.
- Fisking
  To fisk a piece of work means to go through it point by point, often vehemently disagreeing with its contents. The term arose from such treatment meted out to the work of *Independent* journalist Robert Fisk, whose work has been deconstructed regularly by warbloggers.
- Google bomb
  Google bombing is a method of catapulting a website – often a weblog – to the top of a Google search for a given phrase, achieved by abusing a loophole in the search engine's algorithm. Because Google will often recommend sites which do not contain the exact phrase you are looking for, but have been linked to by sites that use that phrase, website owners found they could create pages full of links to their site, often using bizarre and irrelevant keywords, to bring their sites to the top of certain searches.
- Linklog
  A weblog carrying only a simple list of interesting links, without extensive commentary or illustration. Sometimes a linklog will run alongside fuller journal entries or other commentary.
- Moblog
  A weblog created via mobile phone or personal digital assistant (PDA), rather than a computer. These typically feature photographs of the author's travels, and brief text commentary.
- Permalink
  Because a weblog's front page changes regularly, old posts eventually 'fall off' the front page and go into the archives. To make it easier to link back to old posts, weblog services give each post its own unique URL. If you ever link to a specific weblog post, you should use this URL rather than simply 'myweblog.co.uk', so readers will always be able to find the post to which you are referring. The permalink URL for a post can usually be found in a link next to the post, denoted by a #, 'permalink' or 'link'.
- Photoblog
  A weblog composed mainly, or all, of photographs.

- Post
  This is a new blog or piece that is written on your personal site.
- RSS
  Experts differ on whether RSS stands for RDF Site Summary (RDF stands for Resource Description Framework), Really Simple Syndication or Rich Site Summary, but the meaning is the same. RSS is an XML format originally developed by Netscape that is used by many weblogs to syndicate their content.
- Technorati
  Another web service that tracks the content of weblogs (see Blogdex). Its search facility is particularly useful for webloggers anxious to see who is linking to their site, and what they're saying. The site also sports a top 100 weblogs, ranked by inbound links.
- Trackback
  A system devised to make it easier to track conversations between weblogs. So: I write something on my weblog. You want to respond on your weblog, so you write your piece, post it, and send a Trackback 'ping' to my site to, in effect, say, 'hey, I've commented on your piece'. At that point, my weblog automatically links to your comments. And so on.
- Videoblog
  The latest form of blog that streams video clips.
- Warblogger
  A warblogger is a person who runs a weblog that started around or was significantly influenced by the events of 11 September 2001.
- Weblog
  The definition of a weblog is, 'pages consisting of several posts or distinct chunks of information per page, usually arranged in reverse chronology from the most recent post at the top of the page to the oldest post at the bottom'
- XML
  XML is a way of labelling online content to allow computers to understand better what that content is. In a weblogging context, XML underpins the RSS format, which is in turn used to distribute headline feeds to aggregators.

Videoblogs or vlogs

Out of the blogosphere has come the videoblog or vlog. It was an inevitable move towards making it possible for bloggers to upload photos and then video onto their sites.

A vlog is a video that is linked to a blog post (or weblog) and run by an aggregator or feed software that you download. It has grown in popularity since Apple Video iPod was launched and through the availability of iTunes Store's video content. iTunes uses the term video podcast to describe a video blog. Just one of the sites that helps you create a vlog is freevlog.org. You need a video camera to record a video, then pc software to edit it before you upload it onto your blog. Then anyone with RSS feed software is able to download it and watch it. Dedicated vloggers believe that videoblogging will transform the web. The logic is that video is the preferred medium, which is backed up by media surveys. Also, as discussed under the broadcasting section in this chapter, it is already clear that user-generated video is in demand by new independent channels. Think of Gore's Current TV site and the explosion of alternative news channels that cannot be far behind.

The history of videoblogs is short, in that it developed within a rapid eighteen months in the US. In June 2004, Peter Van Dijck and Jay Dedman started the Yahoo Videoblogging Group, which became the focus for vloggers. During the second half of 2004, the national media discovered videoblogging, with articles in the New York Times and a few other American newspapers. In September 2004, iPodderX, the first desktop video aggregator, was released, and in December mefeedia.com was the first vlog directory to use an aggregator. In January 2005 VloggerCon, the first videoblogger conference, was held in New York City, and ANT (now FireAnt) was released. In February 2005, FreeVlog, a step-by-step guide to setting up a videoblog using free tools and services, was launched. In May 2005, vlog.dir.com, the videoblog directory was launched. In June 2005 the Yahoo Videoblogging Group grew to over 1,000 members. A month later Vlogmap.org launched using Google Maps and Google Earth to display vloggers worldwide. In October 2005 Apple announced the 5G iPod able to play video and that iTunes Store would serve video content. In January 2006 Google announced its Video Store.

PRblogs or plogs

As a VJ, you can provide video for broadcast, for mobiles and of course as vlogs, but the commercial application is there too. One of the growth areas for the use of new media is in marketing and PR, or public relations. The PRblog, with or without video, was always going to happen because if you imagine a vast hall with tens of thousands of people in it, talking about a company and its products, that is the power of blogging and companies decided they could not afford to be outside that chat room. The consensus now is that it is too risky to stay out. Why? Well a single blog is unlikely to raise interest or controversy, but when linked to potentially millions of similar ones, it can. A huge 'Chinese whispers' chain can prove positive or negative. It can force organisations into action: product recalls, sackings of staff or politicians; create front page newspaper stories; and push the media agenda. One example is Kryptonite, an American company manufacturer of bicycle locks. It was forced into a costly product recall when a rumour about its faulty design circulated in the blogosphere, and appeared in the newspapers. The company was dealing with the problem on an individual basis, but bloggers forced their hand with consumer pressure. What other marketplace is so fecund, when a blog is created every second? Special search engines like Blogpulse, Technorati, Bloglines, IceRocket, Feedster, Rojo, Blinkx and PubSub now track content . Search for 'alternative fuels', for example, and you'll find opinions, facts and a mix of corporate and personal blogs.

So a PR corporate blog can be part of the Blogosphere, encouraging interaction, informing and branding. The blog monitoring company, Market Sentinel, found in May 2005 no FTSE100 company had a corporate blog. CEO Mark Rogers reckoned that the UK blue chip companies were missing a trick:

> When customers or partners do a search on a company or brand name they are as likely to find a negative comment as they are to find the company's own message. The big UK companies need to get blogging.

While the UK is now climbing on the blog bandwagon, in the US, where they are usually quicker to adapt to new technology and concepts, blogs have revolutionised corporate communications for Fortune 500 companies like Disney, Avon, FedEx, Motorola and McGraw Hill. An increasing number of corporations realise that, with over 30 per cent of Americans using blogs for news, it is vital to engage this technology. Creating a blog is the easy part; finding the right corporate 'voice' is harder. Deciding on the content is also difficult; it needs careful thinking through as to aims and outcomes. What are the benefits? Well, it stimulates feedback, which in turn results in higher search engine rankings, shows the sympathetic 'voice' of a company who knows about its products, and is inexpensive. Blogs can be added to the corporate website as part of an overall online communication strategy. Think of a PRblog or plog as a new e-PR tool, a way forward for the organisation or company to be heard in the global chat room.

Podcasting

The term podcasting was invented by Dannie J. Gregoire, who registered the domain name podcasting.com in 2004. You have probably already listened to podcasts online, when you go to music, entertainment or news websites and you are offered the chance to listen to an audio file. It is a simple technology whereby when you click on the loudspeaker symbol you are setting in motion via an aggregator or RSS feed access to the website where the audio file is stored. There is no direct link to Apple's iPod, despite the name, but of course the company has been clever in responding fast and offering podcast downloads for iPod users. You can then listen to the material away from your computer at your leisure. Many media providers now allow for downloading of podcast material onto your pc or MP3 or other player. Of course you can record a personal voice recording and send it via e-mail to a colleague or friend. It can then be opened using Real Player or other software and saved or played immediately. The easiest way to think of a podcast is like an audio e-mail attachment. It can be radio on demand. You do not have to have an iPod to listen to a podcast. Podcasting gives far more options in terms of content and programming than radio does. Listeners can determine the time and the place, meaning they decide what programming they want to receive and when they want to listen to it. The podcast can also be used for storing and re-playing all sorts of content: talk shows, music shows, interviews, story telling, tutorials, directions, commentaries and sports-casts. It is incredibly simple to podcast as there are a number of different software programmes that allow you to record audio files. Some of them are specific in their content application. Replay Radio allows you to record hundreds of radio broadcasts from all over the world, listen whenever you want on your pc, CD player or MP3 player, and even skip over the fluff. Mix Craft lets you record and mix music for podcasts, and produce podcasts, editing the audio for very little cost. Text Aloud allows instant podcasts with text to speech software; simply type or paste in text, and save as an MP3 for instant podcasting. The applications for podcasts are of course endless, like videos, for education, information, entertainment, news, promotion and of course music content. They are seen as a part of every corporate and news provider's website. The way you can get all sorts of information delivered to you on your mobile phone or e-mail and to are able to download from various sites, is RSS.

RSS or really simple syndication

RSS has really revolutionised the way information can be fed; for companies wanting to keep their clients or employees or just registered users in the loop, it is a quick, easy corporate communication channel. It stands for the really simple syndication system. It customises your web surfing – and that includes blogs. You just choose a newsreader, like bloglines, and the rest is easy, with you even being given alerts when new material like sports results come in. You have probably already signed up for RSS feeds without realising, because lots of websites give you the opportunity of tailoring the information you want to receive in this way: from news providers to anyone offering weather, travel or other information content. If you have not done this yet, go online and look for the RSS sign and sign up for something and see how it is done. You then need to check your e-mail and see what content appears. This is the fastest way to learn – by application. While RSS began as a means to deliver news headlines, it has quickly become a powerful medium to disseminate all kinds of information. In fact it is one of those mechanisms no one can now believe did not exist before.

The RSS feeds are read using a tool referred to as a news aggregator, or an RSS reader. The aggregator periodically checks to see if the RSS feed has been updated. As the feed is updated, new information will automatically appear in the RSS reader. RSS 2.0 is the definitive standard, because of its support for the enclosure tag. This allows a link to a file. The file can be just about anything. So a business can add tutorials, streamed audio lectures, PDF proposals, PowerPoint presentations, podcasts of sales meetings, or advertising portfolios. Think of how you could send PDF documents, meeting agenda notes or any documentation, allowing the receiver to access information without having to deal with cumbersome e-mail attachments. PowerPoint presentations can be distributed more easily in a feed enclosure. So if you're making a presentation you can do it from an iPod or similar hand-held that reads RSS feeds. Video or streaming video is possible via the enclosure field. So news material, lectures or even political debates can be viewed. Audio content or podcasts, as we have discussed, can be sent too. Images can be delivered in the same way, so for example estate agents can use the enclosure field to display photos of homes to interested buyers. They can carry a catalogue with them to show potential buyers at a moment's notice, via their iPod or hand-held device. A company's IT department, in a large corporation especially, can put their own software updates, including zip files, in the enclosure field. This enables users to update the software at a convenient time.

You can set up RSS feeds yourself, you just need to get your own aggregator, choosing from the list below, and any new ones that emerge. The most popular and recommended are: MyYahoo! (web-based aggregator), Bloglines (web-based aggregator), NetNewsWire (Mac), Firefox (browser with integrated RSS features), NewsGator (web-based aggregator and Microsoft Outlook integrated aggregator), FeedDemon (desktop aggregator), Pluck (IE integrated RSS aggregator), SharpReader (desktop aggregator) and YouSubscribe (MSOutlook integrated aggregator).

To give you some examples of how companies are using RSS: Amazon. com is using it to announce their bestsellers and to help their users keep track of releases they are most interested in. FindSavings.com uses RSS to deliver savings coupons and related information. Lockergnome uses RSS to provide visitors with the latest downloads and relevant software. Other companies are using RSS to deliver product updates and patches directly to their customers, just as soon as they become available. A few hundred content publishers are using RSS to deliver audio content, such as MP3 interviews, 'radio' shows and even audio messages, to their customers. Textamerica.com allows people to post pictures, videos and text from their mobile phones and then makes this content available via RSS feeds. Companies are using RSS to deliver White Papers and other educational content. One company uses RSS as a consulting billing awareness tool. The consultants create activity reports and the RSS feeds from the activity channels carry the billable information to the accounting staff for invoice preparation. Many internet publishers are using RSS to deliver their newsletters. Catalogues of products can be sent, with the latest product releases, broken down by the categories the customers are interested in, which makes it easy for them to order. RSS is a facilitator and the best way, so far, of being able to send and receive information of all kinds via broadband, without any limit on the volume of material being sent.

Video streaming

Video streaming is different from pod or vodcasting in that material is sent out *live* or in *real-time*. This means for news organisations, for instance, that they are alerted to material being streamed like live satellite feeds and can then access the material and record it if they so wish. Video streaming for advertising and PR use is immense as it is far less expensive to put up material onto the web than it is to use satellite time and space. It also means that there is no travelling needed, no logistics to organise or people to mobilise, and the video comes directly into a newsroom and can be used or turned around for broadcast immediately. For example, business TV news can use a chief executive's statement on his company's annual results and play it out on audio as well as video. So this means that company results, messages from CEOs and campaigning footage from any NGO (non-governmental organisation), like Oxfam, Save the Children or Greenpeace, can be video streamed online and they just have to alert journalists, members, clients and employees as to the time of the broadcast.

Most organisations use companies who can upload information. Companies like Astream, Syncast or Streamcity. However, it is possible for individuals and companies to upload and stream video via websites themselves and will become commonplace as the call for live video grows.

Texting or SMS messaging

Text messaging, or Short Message Service (SMS), is about to explode in the US. Over 165 million Americans now use mobile phones capable of sending and receiving SMS messages. Domestic SMS traffic is more than tripling annually – making the US the largest growth market for SMS. How is it used? Well the most interesting political use has been by Israel, who literally waged war by text message as it stepped up attacks on Hezbollah guerrillas in Lebanon. Lebanese civilians' mobile phones in July 2006 were being bombarded with messages and voicemails telling civilians to leave areas earmarked for bombardment or risk being killed. Softer use can be by companies from news organisations offering news headlines, sports results and so on, to the tourism and travel industry. It can give instant updates on travel facts. For example, a ski resort could send an early morning SMS notification saying fresh powder snow had fallen overnight, driving more guests to the slopes sooner. Or, at a summer resort, golfers could be alerted at the last minute to tee times that remain open. Seaside venues could fire off SMS surf and weather reports; casino guests could opt into receiving live play updates. Customers sign up for it and so create a database for PR messaging.

Text messaging dovetails with other online promotions such as loyalty points and special offers via opt-in e-mail. In hospitality and tourism communications, SMS adds a new and valuable channel to the multimodal spectrum.

(David LaPlante, CEO of Twelve Horses,
a South African media company)

As a new media device it provides one of the most distinctive opportunities for businesses to forge customer relationships and loyalty. Why? The key role of text messaging in reaching customers is to deliver timely messages, answers to questions, alerts that offer loyal customers short-term discounts, and so on. SMS generally has the best chance of all communication channels of reaching customers instantly, regardless of location. The opportunities for delivering information in this way are virtually endless. It is up to you, the end receiver, to determine what level of service you are looking for, so that you are not bombarded with unwanted messages. Like RSS feeds, you can decide on what sort of information you want, like travel updates about the London Underground service or the motorways, or sports results information.

Before we leave behind these new applications it is worth looking at one sector where a boom is about to happen. Marketing and PR is a sector that has traditionally liaised with the media. Why? Because it needs to promote its clients and their products and services. So the changes in viewing habits and the move to using broadband and new media should be incorporated in their strategies. While video streaming and webcasting has become an acceptable or standard means of delivering information, many PR companies and PR practitioners have ignored the new media possibilities. It has been their clients who have pushed for them, as the news media have published and discussed blogging and podcasting, for example. The implications for broadcast PR are clear: with more than 200,000 British homes hooking up to broadband each month and consumers increasingly opting to view video and audio content on their mobiles and online, these new media are emerging as essential in an overall broadcast PR strategy.

The PR industry thinks of radio as being the hardware unit by which you listen. It thinks of video as being for TV. But why can't this content be broadcast via a website? It may not reach the millions of viewers you get with the early evening news, but you will reach a more targeted audience. Getting the chief executive or CEO on FT.com, for example, can be very valuable.

(Howard Kosky, managing director of broadcast agency
Markettiers4dc.)

PR organisations are missing a trick, says Stuart Maister, founder of broadcast communications agency BroadView. 'Internet content is editorially driven. It is "pull" content, consumers want to see it, as opposed to "push" content, which is advertising'. The BBC with its multi-platform approach is one he believes companies should emulate. There is also the potential to develop brand-related editorial for news and lifestyle portals. Online media owners, such as Tiscali and Lycos, are keen to receive brand-related content. Tiscali portal director Richard Ayers says his company recently partnered with Sony to produce content on digital photography for its technology channel. Ayers points out that in this environment, brand promotion through editorial is acceptable: 'Overt brand promotion is a question of tone. If it's done knowingly, cleverly or with humour, then you can get away with a high level of brand promotion'. Well, until regulating the web happens, something that is even now being discussed by the European Union. Until then the web allows companies to upload their own videos and programmes. The advantage over TV is the direct control you have over the message. If you are a brand sponsoring a factual TV programme, you are not allowed to get involved with the content. But what is to stop, for example, B&Q producing its own content on DIY projects online, such as how to put up a shelf, and selling tools and material at the same time?

Food for thought, because producing content for online use requires video operators and those capable of writing and producing scripts too – in other words, VJs. This is a huge growth area and one that opens up career possibilities.

Conclusion

New media have opened up a whole range of new internet communication tools, using broadband. The best thing about them is that most are easy to use so that anyone can establish their own blog, podcast, videocast or even RSS feed. All you have to have is the will to do it. That is if it is for personal use, but as this chapter has shown many of the tools are now being applied to the commercial world too. That is inevitable, as they streamline and speed up the process in every field of communication. Let us close the chapter with the thoughts of one VJ pioneer now excited by the new media possibilities:

> my fascination at the moment is blogging technology, also the way that video technology can connect people for video dialogue. Look at Bloggingheadstv, where bloggers with webcams debate on a split screen and then record it for us to watch. It is TV not as we know it. Or take Bloggit where you can buy a green screen and get your own newsroom. We need to train a new type of journalist to make sure they're fully aware of technology and what it can do.
>
> (Dan Damon)

Questions for students

1   What has propelled the growth of new media?
2   Which is the most dominant of the new media tools being used?
3   What are the benefits of new media, and for whom?
4   Is the marketing and PR sector using these e-tools?
5   How does a VJ have to encompass new media for work?

8   The future of videojournalism

A multi-media future was confirmed in 2006 when three journalistic markers were put down pointing the way for things to come. First of all, for the first time the Pulitzer Prize (America's top journalistic annual award) for Commentary in 2006 was given to a multi-media journalist Nicholas D. Kristof who works for the *New York Times*. His videos, articles and blogs all appear in the newspaper's online version. Second, *Time Magazine*, as mentioned in the last chapter, for its prestigious Person of the Year award named not an individual, but *you* – that is, us the general public for our contributions to the web and 'making them matter'. Or as *Time*'s editorial put it, for 'seizing the reins of the global media, for founding and framing the new digital democracy, for working for nothing and beating the pros at their own game'. Third, what is being called the 'YouTube effect', following the CNN effect when it helped launch 24 hour rolling news, is being hailed as the way forward for user-generated content on an unprecedented global scale. The website that caught the world's attention and imagination as a portal is being rated as inspirational and a force for the future of the individual and independent's view of the world. All three are US events, but seeing as this is the birthplace of the internet maybe it is not surprising. Certainly categories for online achievements are now being incorporated into journalistic awards by UK organisations.

Trying to predict the future is a tricky business at the best of times and even harder when it comes to new technology. It is moving very fast, but what is true is that the time appears to have arrived for videojournalism and that, as has been documented in this book, in every part of the media, video and visuals are seen as a prerequisite. What has not developed yet is a strong cadre of freelance VJs to service the media, but gradually organisations are training people at work and some of these will no doubt move into the independent sphere to work.

Vaughan Smith of Frontline News, always one to champion the independent journalist and VJ, is developing an internet channel that he says,

> Will do away with the need to be involved with the mainstream. You won't have to call the evening news editor to see if the programme will

take your footage, you can just put it on the internet. Then the audience will judge on whether it is interesting and agencies may check on value of footage or stories and offer to pay for the usage or distribution, or not.

Smith is repeating what is becoming a mantra for those internet channel entrepreneurs who are talking and reaching out to the consumer, the internet user and above all the video maker. He, together with Gore and countless other new media players, is arguing from the independents' and freelancers' standpoint, challenging the national and established news providers. Terry Heaton, a promoter of videojournalism and VJs for years, feels he can see into his crystal ball and believes that the prospects for VJs will increase because

> people will switch to alternative news channels in sufficient numbers to watch independent VJs' reports, as long as they know what the agenda is of the journalist or the provider. In much the same way as bloggers in the US especially, but also in the UK, have become identified with certain viewpoints and political associations, the same pattern will develop where you would choose a 'known' environmentalist VJ site, for example, to watch.

The Yahoo! website has a dedicated VJ, or 'sojo' as he calls himself. Kevin Sites is the solo journalist/cameraman who is covering every conflict globally for Yahoo!'s website and his HotZone page. Yahoo! has an estimated 400 million users and around 2 million hit Kevin's page (hotzone.yahoo.com) monthly. He and his team of three, who do their own work too, offer reports in different formats: short documentaries, photo essays, video interviews or written dispatches. The idea was to offer a more human or personal view on foreign conflicts to a US audience who are not renowned for being interested in global events beyond their borders. Yahoo! profits by getting a better image or profile (which it needs after it identified two Chinese dissident journalists for the Chinese government which resulted in their imprisonment). The interesting point is that Yahoo! is not a news organisation nor does it approve or decide on the stories that are covered, yet it still deems this worthwhile to carry on its site. There is no reason why oil companies, for example, may not decide too that environmental videos are a bonus for their websites and images. Only the tip of the video iceberg has so far been seen. Vaughan Smith agrees,

> broadband internet broadcasting is what we're going to be doing, so that a Chinaman or someone in the Australian outback or Zimbabwe can put a report on our site and can go directly to an audience. It takes away the need to be involved with the mainstream, you don't have to call the evening news editor to try and sell it, and you can just put it on. Things like water-printing pieces to stop them being stolen are now possible and

we'll still use small format cameras. It is over to the audiences to decide whether anything is interesting, they will be the judges, not the agencies or broadcasters. Broadcasters are, in my opinion, arrogant and have developed this culture of superiority. I want to see journalism delivered efficiently, without complications and I am sure the market will come.

Going by the recent survey of TV audience trends, Smith is right that if your interest is in say, saving the bat, and someone has a bat watch protection site with video clips and information, then you will watch it. More than that you are likely to add it to your online favourites list and perhaps ask for downloads and content to your mobile or e-mail. Any one of you who has clicked on the news pages and home pages of servers to get a news update would agree that you have already done away with someone directing you as to what to watch and that you now choose your own reports to open or run, according to your interests. You mark the websites you want in your favourites column; you also sign up for RSS feeds from a number of different servers of information of all kinds that satisfy your interests, be they sport, fashion, gossip or the weather. It is, remember, what *Time* calls, 'our' space and is being developed as such by individuals, groups and corporations alike.

Rick Thompson now of T-media, but before that a BBC TV foreign editor from 1978–82, and then in 1994 editor of newsgathering for BBC World Service and BBC World, also believes that

most broadcast news organisations have been surprisingly slow in exploiting the benefits of digital technology and therefore videojournalism in its various forms. For a dynamic industry full of talented individuals, it is difficult to understand why it is often so conservative. Cameramen often say, 'these little cameras aren't professional!'. That's crazy. They produce very good pictures and sound and are much easier to carry around and use, and are less intrusive. It is like saying, 'I am now going to make an important phone call, so I will need a very big phone!' And these small cameras are much cheaper than conventional Beta SP shooting kits. The benefits to a news programme of having twice as many cameras on the road each day would be great. All TV journalists today should be trained to edit their own material on computers as a matter of course. Many people, including teenagers, are doing it at home already! It is fast and relatively simple. As for shooting their own material, that poses different problems. I am sure there will be many more VJs shooting their own material in just a few years. But I can't imagine the BBC's Washington correspondent or political editor being asked to shoot his or her own pictures. There will always be a need for the core two–person team of a correspondent working closely with a multi-skilled camera operator, who can get the shots while the reporter is getting the facts. But there will certainly be lots more single-operators, not only in local newsrooms, but working abroad, and shooting, editing and voicing topical features. I think *diversity* is the future. There will be rough-and-ready shooting and editing; there will be many more videos posted by individuals on the web. But there will also be 'classic' news coverage for many many years to come.

This leads to the question that is being put to every Chief Executive in UK TV, which is, 'Does digital mean the death of traditional broadcasting?' Below are some responses.

Linear channels will remain the most important thing but they're no longer going to be sufficient. A combination of smaller channels, new platforms and time shifting via PVR or broadband will change the landscape very significantly. For some audiences and channels those things matter very little.

(Andy Duncan, Chief Executive, Channel 4)

We appear to be moving into a world where everything is provided for free. The premise is based on advertisers being there to support things. But if the audiences do move off to Bebo or YouTube then that is going to make it difficult if the revenue follows them.

(Janice Hughes, Chief Executive, Spectrum Consultants)

Hughes is right that although all this change is fuelled by investment, traditionally advertising has supported the commercial media. Although the start-up costs for internet channels are much cheaper than for starting a satellite channel or 24 hours news channel broadcasting terrestrially, the funding still has to be found. TV has until recently been seen by advertisers as having a captive audience watching their 'must-see' programmes and so an obvious target. The rapid change from single to multi-media platforms has found the advertisers unsure of their strategies and undecided whether to swap old for new media. A good example of this is a website called heavy. com that is a broadband network where users swap videos and games and also offers male-oriented content. It has captured an 18–34-year-old male age group that advertisers covet. As a result the large brand names like Sony, Diesel, Nike and Axe have started advertising on the site and its revenue has risen a staggering 300 per cent in one year from 2005. Now that access to the consumer can no longer be controlled by the broadcasters and cable station operators, the advertisers are set to follow where the consumer leads them. That path is determined by the content on websites or internet broadcasting channels that offers what people want. It is also a case of the websites like Google being able to process user data and so attract advertisers who can be placed appropriately on pages, or Amazon which has expanded its services by watching what its online customers want and buy. If Google continues to generate the same proportion of its revenue from the UK it will have netted,

Andy Duncan predicts, $1.57 billion, or £790 million, in 2006 alone and will overtake ITV as the single largest recipient of advertising money within two years. Could this be the news that UK companies need to shake them up and look to their investments online? It is a change in dynamic and while no one forecasts the demise of commercial TV, there is an undeniable logic that if the advertising declines so does the traditionally-delivered service. As with all change, there is no going back. Advertisers are aware of this, as are public relations companies who advise business on where and how to access the media.

Alex Graham, Chief Executive, Wall to Wall TV, is impatient at even entertaining the idea of TV's demise,

> I think that every time there is a new technology people predict the death of the old one, but movies didn't kill off newspapers, television didn't kill off the cinema, video didn't kill off television and nor did DVDs and the internet will not kill off television networks either.

The Head of Sky News appointed in late 2006, John Ryley, agrees with Graham and from Sky's 24-hour news perspective, and its position within Rupert Murdoch's global media empire, Ryley is optimistic:

> I still can't predict with 100 per cent certainty what the future holds for television news. It's very tempting to recall what the Chinese leader Chou En-lai said about the French Revolution, and argue that 'it is too early to say' what impact the internet and new media will have on 24-hour news channels. Tempting but blithe and blinkered because the internet is made for breaking news. Some media watchers believe the internet's speed and immediacy will destroy 24-hour news channels. They are missing a trick. Twenty-four hour news and the internet are not mutually exclusive. Both rolling news and on-demand news will grow. And here's why: if we, or the BBC, were just to run a news channel on its own it might end up being bypassed. But all of us are pushing as aggressively as we can to supply customers with bespoke content via the technology of their choice at a time of their choice.
>
> The growth of new media offers business and money-making opportunities. Mobile phones are a vital new outlet: tens of thousands of subscribers are paying to see a package featuring live streaming of Sky News. Over the next five years it is our biggest opportunity. The channel is committed to a spirit of innovation hour by hour, day by day, and adopts an entrepreneurial mindset.

However upbeat Ryley is, not even he can be sure of what future changes in technology might mean. One of the most important will be when a pc will have a large enough capacity to show the same digital quality images as TV. It can then take over from the conventional TV set. Another prediction is for

Freeview to overtake satellite as the most popular way to watch TV in the UK by 2008, according to Datamonitor.

The digital switchover from analogue will happen in 2007. The UK already has the world's highest level of digital TV viewers at nearly 70 per cent, the broadcasting regulator Ofcom revealed early in 2006. The US is second with 55 per cent, but no other European country has passed 50 per cent. The Cumbrian town of Whitehaven will be first to lose its analogue signal in the UK in 2007, with the switchover process due to be completed by 2012.

In terms of the camera technology for VJs and camera people, the future is tape-less cameras. These are already available but the cards holding information are limited in capacity. However, they do have interesting features like continuous recording for two hours. So if you are waiting for something to happen, you leave the camera going and it keeps recording until any action happens. As Andy Benjamin of the BBC's DV Solutions section explains, the new cameras help filming of programmes:

> I trained the camera people for the series 'Strictly Come Dancing' and they were stopping and starting the cameras. This created problems in editing, so now they just keep running and it is all stored, because it is so cheap and costs less than having an editor trying to match sequences for hours. It also means that you never miss the action this way; you don't have to tell the viewers in commentary or with a presenter to camera about how one dancer broke their ankle – you have it on tape.

The BBC's technology department are working on the 'perfect' camcorder, made to specifications that the programme-makers and the self-op journalists want. They came up with all sorts of requests, as Benjamin describes:

> Some wanted a camera in two parts with a separate recording section that could be as slim as an iPod and fit into a pocket to keep the camera weight down, also a separate hard drive that could also be separate to the camera. We gave the concept of a new camcorder to all the manufacturers asking if they would make one and Panasonic agreed. So hopefully in a couple of years we'll see an easy to use, high quality, light camera that has better lenses, better ergonomically positioned switches and buttons, viewing screens and is weather- proof. It also has to produce content that is easily uploadable to any system and can contain meta-data on recordings.

Meta-tags are a way of identifying material that show on the tape in editing and tell who shot the material, date, time, location, music and who owns the rights. It is the future for archives and for organisations like the BBC, ITV or NBC who have committed themselves to opening their film archives to public use for downloading. Footage not in the company's copyright will then show up and be excluded. The biggest expense will be in transferring material onto a searchable database that can be digitally stored.

Newspapers online

The news environment is changing fast, as media mogul Rupert Murdoch warned recently, with newspaper editors presiding over a decaying industry so that they must face up to the internet or perish! This is advice from the man who has put his money where his mouth is and spent £315 million acquiring MySpace.com as part of his own internet strategy. He has a projected income in 2007 of between £175–350 million from the online businesses of NewsCorp, his holding company. Watchers of the Murdoch newspaper empire in the UK would argue that he had no choice as the sales figures continue to disappoint. However, MySpace is already being turned into a bi-media or multi-media resource, by tapping into its user-generated content to produce a print issue of UK style magazine *Marmalade* for March 2007. There is little doubt that newspapers' immediate and future challenge is to stem the flow of print readers and re-direct them to their branded online sites. Certainly Web 2.0 has made new technology a reality for many consumers, and digital newsrooms for newspapers already exist both in the UK and the US, as well as Asia. It is anticipated that the next big upgrade, when the internet can allow for 8 Mb downloads of high quality video, will bring even greater possibilities.

Murdoch's warning may be timely, a wake-up call to some newspaper owners, but the demise of the newspaper is not yet apparent. The latest survey from the US where trends are usually significant for the UK's future development shows that 39 of the top 40 daily newspapers in the US already use video on their sites, according to a recent study by online-clip distributor The News Market. Of 150 print publications surveyed, 79 per cent are capable of producing video. 'Both newspapers and TV stations need to have video to be competitive online', says web consultant Steve Safran, president of Safran Media Group. 'The goal is to provide the best local news in a multimedia format'. While the UK has the highest numbers of broadband users in Europe, there are 52 million US homes with high-speed broadband, which allows video viewing at a quality comparable to that of TV. So the battle is on, with newspapers still the online first choice for news. US newspapers are working hard to keep it that way; for example, one newspaper *The Virginia Pilot* in December 2005, launched HamptonRoads.tv, a portal with local video and AP clips on national and international news. It has also to compete with local TV news and hopes to appeal to the disaffected 18 to 34 age group that wants something different. 'We're focussed on a younger generation that is disconnected with local media', says Chris Kouba, the site's online-content manager. On a larger scale the *New York Times* has turned its website, NYTimes.com, into a veritable multi-media feast. It has five dedicated videojournalists producing packages, and many reporters out with dv cameras. Since offering videos in December 2005, more than 700 video reports have been uploaded and the site counts 4–5 million video streams per month. 'The website is about delivering journalism in the best medium we can', says NYTimes.com general manager Vivian Schiller. 'Some stories cry out for video; text and video together are a powerful combination'.

Their success is not just the number of hits to their sites but the amount of advertising that they can attract to boost income. This too is happening as video ads in the US are increasing. According to Merrill Lynch, broadband-ad spending is projected to reach $25 billion, that's around £12.5 billion, by 2009. At the moment, one research firm, Borrell and Associates, says newspapers online are beating TV sites and earned some £1 billion in online advertising revenue in 2005 alone.

In the UK the move to the internet by newspapers has been slower but 2006 saw a change in pace. Most national newspaper groups have finally acknowledged that being online is not only a necessity but can also be profitable too. My cursory survey of websites shows that *The Times* has video news clips supplied by Reuters, but not highly visible on their website, The Sun runs clips but still points online readers to the newspaper. Associated Newspapers' *The Daily Mail* has a multi-media website and so does The Mirror Group. While *The Daily Telegraph* has gone for a total makeover. Will Lewis, the newly appointed editor, is leading an operation that has cost the Barclay Brothers, who recently bought the newspaper group, millions of pounds. It has switched to becoming a multi-media operation, with staff filing not only print stories for the newspaper, but also material for online and changing web stories during the day, plus doing podcasts and vodcasts too. Reader research apparently showed an appetite for receiving news in different ways, and this convinced management to take the plunge. *The Telegraph* reports that readers prefer their news information in the form of: text in the morning on the web, on their mobiles or in print; video at lunchtime; audio in the afternoon; and a 'click and carry', pdf document for the journey home. While this sounds like a dream scenario and there are as yet no statistics to prove its success, it does mean that multi-skilled or production journalists and the re-training of existing ones are needed to deliver to the various different resource desks: online, video and audio as well as print. Video journalists are to be appointed too. ITN will provide video content for the website featuring some of the newspaper's best-known journalists. 'Our partnership with ITN, one of the best-known names in television news, and the launch of Telegraph PM [the multimedia edition] demonstrate our commitment to being at the cutting edge of the new media age', Says Edward Roussel, Telegraph Group Online Editorial Director. The acknowledged explosion in broadband internet access is stirring up traditionally run newspaper groups everywhere.

The UK nationals and regional newspaper groups are not far behind, using their journalism sense, as in one example, to know what makes a good news piece, be it in print or on video. North Wales Newspapers uploaded video footage onto their websites for the first time in October 2006, showing readers two motorcyclists speeding at 100 mph. along the A55 road. It was taken from the weekly blog written by North Wales Police Chief Richard Brunstrom showing the riders on the main route along the North Wales coast. They were filmed travelling erratically at 100 mph from a helicopter, before being arrested and later banned for 12 and 15 months. For the newspaper group's publishing director Graham Breeze, it was a case of good timing as

> we were developing our sites and were actively looking for the right material to launch video streaming. The antics of speeding motorcyclists through our publishing area is of concern to all our readers, particularly with the number of fatalities on our roads this summer.

The local stories are supplied by their own journalists, with the regional and national ones often by the Associated Press Online Video Network . *The Hull Daily Mail* in the north of England introduced in 2006 video reports onto its website after sending six print journalists off on the UK Press Association's new videojournalism course. 'We are experimenting with putting videos of local news stories on our website ... because people want to access news in different ways and increasingly want to use the web. We have to respond to that', Paul Hartley, deputy editor, said in an interview at the launch. Yet another example is the Johnston Press, a regional newspaper group. It is set to do a trial run in 2007 from its Preston newsroom that produces the *Lancashire Evening Post*, with a roll-out to around 70 offices nationwide. The Preston newsroom has been reorganised so its 50 journalists can file video reports for streaming on the newspaper's website. A revamped news editing operation coordinates rolling news coverage across the internet, mobile phones and newspaper. Lancashire Evening Post staff were reported to be happy to act as videojournalists. Interestingly the newspaper group spokesman did not believe that the BBC's local TV plans would damage them, while other newspaper groups, where the pilot for local TV has been carried out, have acknowledged that they have lost readers to local TV, watched over the internet. Finally *The Yorkshire Post*, and more than 300 other newspaper titles in its group, is converting 70 newsrooms into multimedia operations that file video reports as well as written stories on their websites.

Confirmation of the increased use of streaming video and audio by news organisations online comes from a company called TheNewsMarket. According to Shoba Purushothaman, co-founder, president and CEO, it delivers video clips to 5,000 newsrooms in 140 countries online, including the BBC, Reuters and Associated Press. 'We aggregate video clips for broadcast, online and even print journalists. Traditional broadcast journalists used to be the only ones to use video but the websites of Forbes, Fortune and Business-Week all incorporate video now', says Purushothaman. Organisations such as the US State Department and the UK Ministry of Defence pay TheNews-

Market for supplying B-roll footage and VNRs to journalists, who access them for free. Footage from Iraq has proved particularly popular, along with healthcare and technology stories, adds Purushothaman. The newly-formed Associated Press Online Video Network is another ad-supported news video service that draws on the global newsgathering resources of The Associated Press and its network of members to provide video summaries of breaking news stories for websites. The Online Video Network offers video clips covering national, international, entertainment, technology and business news.

Using a recognised brand is working to the newspapers' strength and history with a readership and audience. So they have not got to establish or promote their names in the way that any start-up site has to do. The US has seen papers accelerating in developing their websites into multi-media ones, spurred on by opportunities to earn advertising revenue. In order to service these online sites, the job definition of the print journalist is undergoing a change. They are being asked and trained to carry with them digital cameras and video cameras, to blog and to send back pictures electronically faster than ever before. Immediate news is expected and demanded by website users. There are dedicated videojournalists too, trained to produce reports as opposed to footage.

As the American executive producer of Studio 55, a half-hour webcast produced by a local newspaper, the *Naples Daily News* in Florida, says, all this sort of innovation is long-term. 'This isn't a bet to have immediate returns in 2006', says Rob Curley. 'This is a bet for 2009'. For at least one broadcast-journalism graduate, the move into video production got her a job presenting and helping produce the newscast. She represents a new style newspaper workforce, where some are being trained, as at *The New York Times* and *Atlanta Journal-Constitution*, to shoot video and others being hired as videographers and 'multimedia' journalists.

So a new equation emerges: the multi-media platforms = more video = increased job opportunities for those with VJ skills.

For mainstream broadcasters fighting a rearguard action against the newspaper video news, the quality argument, they say, remains.

> Standards are lower then they used to be, but there is an issue as to what industry perceives as low standards and the audience perceive they are. The more mundane and prosaic the picture, the higher the quality you need; the more dramatic, the less it matters. For example, no one looked at the film of Concorde crashing and said why didn't you let it go out of frame first....
>
> (Vin Ray, BBC Head of School of Journalism)

The footage was shot by an amateur and it recorded the plane crashing into a hotel close to Charles de Gaulle airport in Paris. They were the only pictures of the event so they were broadcast worldwide. Much like the citizen material being offered or UGC, the occasion demanded the broadcasting, but there is a wider issue here. That is whether the economics and sheer growth of video footage is going to crash through the quality threshold.

John Ive, a former Sony executive, in an interview, is philosophic about this and other changes:

> Yes, broadcasters are challenged by citizen video. Anyone can make technically good video and many are talented. We debate this often. Broadcasters need to 'raise the bar' and differentiate themselves – High Definition is one way. Of course good creative and production skills are necessary not just technology . Almost every country has a different view on what is good enough for news. For example, the Japanese broadcasters NHK use HDCAM [high definition cameras] for news, a format that some other countries are using only for top end drama and movies! In the US many regional news stations work on a tough budget. Remember the VJs pioneered by the cable channel NY1. They gave consumer camcorders to videojournalists who had to shoot and edit their own material which was controversial at the time. Germany uses Digital Betacam for news which is high end for others, whereas in Norway the small consumer dv cameras were used for news until DVCAM became available.

Question: Are tape-less and HD cameras the way it's going?

> HD will become the standard eventually – the norm. The use of tape is gradually reducing but the use of low cost removable media [Sony XDCAM/XDCAMHD, for example] is still important. When you're out shooting in the field, you take a box of tapes or discs to be sure you don't run out. At the moment it is difficult to do this with solid state memory, that the tape-less cameras have, and there is difficulty with short record times and high cost. Also programme makers like to hold material, store it on a shelf, so maybe removable media will have a place for a long time. Unless storage means improve that is.

Conclusion

Having begun this chapter by remarking that making predictions is tricky in the communications sector, there are enough people in the business who are thinking long and hard about change and who are prepared to make changes. Their views are naturally defending their positions and also their communication strategies. Everyone believes that they have taken new media seriously and are trying, if not already incorporating, interactive possibilities in their broadcasting.

This book has been about videojournalism and how to practise it or think about doing so, in a time of change. It provides a useful tour of the state of the media both old and new, where a VJ might work and might find work. This is an exciting period for those in the media, where employers and employees alike are facing challenges to keep up with technology and to provide the services that people want. It is a period of enlightenment and one which will hopefully bring benefits not just to those in Western Europe and the US but to the developing countries where online communication is key to fast-tracking change.

Questions to students

1   What proof is there that multi-media platforms have now been established for print and TV?
2   Why is there a fear that broadcast TV might die out?
3   What have been the major changes in the way newspapers have developed?
4   Does the quality argument about video streamed online hold good?
5   Has the need for VJs increased as a result of change in the media?

Appendix

A GUIDE NEWS-SCRIPT

Running Time: two and a half minutes

COMMENTARY

PICTURES

Scientists at Sheffield University
have developed a 'super' tomato
that they say can protect against cancer

Shots of huge tomato. Shots of
tomatoes being picked and packed.

Professor Avtar Handa SOUNDBITE

Interview with Prof. in his university
greenhouse.

'We were pleasantly surprised to find
that we could increase the nutritional
value of a fruit like the tomato'.

COMMENTARY

Shots of science labs.

Scientists working on both sides of the
Atlantic have managed to do this through
biotechnology, for the first time, as
Professor Handa's co-researcher explains.

Shot of Dr Mattoo walking through a
greenhouse full of tomato plants.

Dr Autar Mattoo SOUNDBITE

Interview with Dr Mattoo.

'By inserting a gene derived from yeast into tomato
plants, an enzyme was produced that resulted
in a substantial increase in the amount of lycopene
in tomatoes. This is the active cancer-fighting
substance'.

Reporter to camera (holding tomato)

PIECE TO CAMERA

'This tomato is coloured red by the
lycopene that is reputed to help protect

against prostate and other forms of cancers,
but the use of GM technology to create
a new super fruit will face opposition'.

COMMENTARY

Fred Gittings of the Natural Food Lobby
is at the forefront of the movement to
keep food in the UK grown by natural
means and preferably organically.

Shots of Fred Gittings working at his
desk.

Fred Gittings SOUNDBITE

Interview with Mr Gittings

'This is just another example of scientists
running away with themselves and creating
products that are artificial and may well
bring some benefits, but we don't really
know what harmful effects there may
be as well. What are they going to dream
up next – a peach that peels itself?
I hope not'.

COMMENTARY

Professor Handa is sure that there are no
negatives to his new super fruit.

Shots of super fruit being picked.

'We expect opposition to come from
different lobby groups, but we really
believe that we're pushing the frontiers
of science forward to the benefit of
people – surely that can't be wrong?'

Reporter to camera

PIECE TO CAMERA

Whatever you think about a new
enriched tomato, it is up to the
Government food agencies to ensure that
we, the consumer, are safeguarded and
that any new product like this is thoroughly
tested before coming to our supermarket
shelves.
This is J. King for BBC News, Sheffield'.

Reporter ends the piece to camera by
walking away to reveal mounds of
super tomatoes.

A running order for a news bulletin

Story slug	Segment	Details	Story Producer	Team Approval	Final Approval	Est Duration	Actual
HEADS	HEAD INTRO- change each hour						
	Top Litvinenko	PRES + TX OOV (oov = video pics)	Fred	12		0.05	0.06
	SOT (soundbite)	SOT (out...poisoning)		12			0
	TOP item	TX OOV (video pics used as underlay)		12			0.07
	2nd FOOD item	WIPE + TX OOV		12		0.1	0.07
	3rd LEBANON	WIPE + TX OOV					0.06
HEAD TEASES	HEAD TEASE SET-UP	ONLY REMOVE IF NO TEASES					0
	TEASE 1	TX OOV					0.09
	TEASE 2	WIPE + TX OOV					0.05
TITLES	PRES NAME AND AASTON	TX TITLES-WS PRES- (this means run titles and wide shot of presenter)					0.12
HEAD INSETS	XXX INSET	LITVINENKO					0
	XXX INSET	NEXT STORY STILL PICTURE					0
	INTRO	SPLIT READ					0.29
LITVINENKO	STORY ITEM	TX NEXT (this means run film next)	John			2.00	2.00
	REPORTER X WESTMINSTER	PRES + 1 (presenter interviews reporter)					0.01
	REPORTER X MOSCOW	PRES + OS MAP + OS DTL					2.15
	TIMELINE GFX (graphics)						2.15
	STILLS	GFX STILLS					0.47
	FLOATS	TX ONLY					0.01
	STORY ASTONS	ASTONS ONLY					0.01
	INSET (this means a still photo of Litvinenko is seen to the side of the presenter)	INSET STILL					0.03
	INTERACTIVE TRAIL						
	WIDOW STATEMENT LIVE						0
	PLAY OUT						0.07
FOOD (next item)	INTRO	PRESENTER					0.04
							0.16

Bibliography

Research for this book has been through interviews with a number of people in the media. All the statistics and other information have been collected over the period of writing this book, appropriately through the internet. I collected newspaper and magazine articles, press releases and technical information to keep up to date with all the new media changes especially. The chapters on filming, news production and new media were revised from my university lectures on these subjects.

People quoted in the text with the name of their organisation can easily be traced online for those wanting to know more about them and their field of interest.

For readers and students wanting to explore the world of broadcast journalism more, I would suggest the following books. Each year working journalists have books published, so it is as well to look on bookshop shelves too.

Suggested reading

S. Adams, *Interviewing for Journalists*, London: Routledge, 2001

C. Alden, *On Air: The Guardian Guide to a Career in TV & Radio*, London: Guardian Books, 2004

S. Allan, *News Culture*, Maidenhead: Open University, 2004

S. Allan and B. Zelizer, *Reporting War*, London: Routledge, 2004

K. Auletta, *Media Man: Ted Turner's Improbable Empire*, New York: W.W. Norton and Co., 2005

J. Baudrillard, *The Gulf War Did Not Take Place*, Indiana University Press, 1995

T. Carlyle, 'Heroes, Hero-Worship and the Heroic in History' Lecture V, 19 May 1840

M. El-Nawawy, *Al-Jazeera: the Story of the Network*, New York: Basic Books, 2003

B. Franklin, *Writing for Broadcast Journalists*, London: Routledge, 2004

M. Horsman, *Sky High – the Rise and Rise of BSkyB*, Mason, OH: Texere Publishing, US, 1998

A. Kitty and R. Greenwald, *Outfoxed: Rupert Murdoch's War on Journalism*, New York: Disinformation company, 2005

R. Lindley, *And Finally ... the History of ITN*, London: Methuen, 2005

David Loyn, *Frontline: The True Story of the British Mavericks Who Changed the Face of War Reporting*, London: Michael Joseph, 2006

H. Miles, *Al Jazeera – How Arab TV News Challenges America*, New York: Grove Press, 2005

V. Ray, *The Television News handbook*, London: Pan, 2003

John Sergeant, *Maggie: Her Fatal Legacy*, London: Pan, 2005

R. Thompson, *Writing for Broadcast Journalists*, London: Routledge, 2004

B. Zelizer, *Journalism after September 11*, London: Routledge, 2002

Personal accounts of broadcast journalism

Martin Bell, *Through Gates of Fire: A Journey into World Disorder*, London: Phoenix, 2004

Michael Buerk, *The Road Taken*, London: Arrow, 2005

Fergal Keane, *All These People: A Memoir*, London: Harper Perennial, 2006

Andrew Marr, *My Trade: A Short History of British Journalism*, London: Pan, 2005

J. Simpson, *News from No-man's Land – Reporting the World*, London: Pan, 2003

J. Simpson, *The Wars Against Saddam: Taking the Hard Road to Baghdad*, London: Pan, 2004

Jon Snow, *Shooting History – a Personal Journey*, London: Harper Perennial, 2005

Index